The Founders' Guide to Corporate Venture Capital

Filling a critical gap that has left founders unprepared for the nuances of corporate venture capital (CVC) engagement, this book provides a definitive, practitioner-focused field guide for navigating this complex world and avoiding pitfalls caused by misaligned incentives, hidden terms, or corporate politics.

With CVCs now participating in over 20% of all venture deals, founders urgently need a playbook that addresses the unique strategic motivations, management structures, and deal terms of these powerful and increasingly common investors. This book is the first written specifically for the founder on how to negotiate with CVCs, focusing particularly on side-letter terms and their long-term and often unforeseen impacts. Written by a practicing CVC investor with deep experience across institutional and corporate VC, it also offers a rare, holistic view of the entire venture ecosystem, enabling readers to understand how a CVC's dual strategic and financial goals predict their behavior, incentives, and potential conflicts of interest.

Through detailed checklists and case studies, this book covers every step of the startup–CVC engagement, from pre-meeting research to post-closing strategy. This book is the definitive resource for startup founders and their executive teams who are actively fundraising or preparing to raise from CVCs, institutional VCs working with CVCs, and for students in MBA, law, and undergraduate business programs interested in a career in startups or CVCs.

Frederick (Freddy) Dopfel is a full-time CVC investor. In 2025, he was named "Corporate VC of the Year" by the Association for Corporate Growth, Silicon Valley. His commentary has appeared in TechCrunch, VentureBeat, and other publications, and he is a frequent speaker to founders, MBA programs, and accelerators. He has invested through LG Technology Ventures, Samsung Ventures, and institutional funds such as Grishin Robotics. He holds an M.S. in Management Science and Engineering from Stanford University and a B.S. in Engineering Physics from UC Berkeley.

The Founders' Guide to Corporate Venture Capital

Navigating Strategic Investment

Frederick C. Dopfel

Routledge
Taylor & Francis Group
NEW YORK AND LONDON

Designed cover image: Getty

First published 2027
by Routledge
605 Third Avenue, New York, NY 10158

and by Routledge
4 Park Square, Milton Park, Abingdon, Oxon, OX14 4RN

Routledge is an imprint of the Taylor & Francis Group, an informa business

ISBN: 9781041282037 (hbk)
ISBN: 9781041282020 (pbk)
ISBN: 9781003758280 (ebk)

DOI: 10.4324/9781003758280

Typeset in Sabon
by codeMantra

Contents

Acknowledgments

This book is a labor of love, and it would not exist without the countless founders, students, and entrepreneurs whose questions inspired it. For years, as both an investor and a speaker, I was asked the same set of questions in meeting after meeting: “How is a CVC different from a regular VC?”, “What is a ‘side letter’ and what should I look out for?”, “Can and should I trust a CVC?”

While foundational texts on venture capital existed, there was no practical, founder-focused playbook for navigating the unique and complex world of corporate investment. This book was written to be that playbook. My greatest thanks go to that community of entrepreneurs; your curiosity and drive are the real origin of this project.

Of course, a project like this is never a solo endeavor. On a personal note, this book would not have been possible without the unwavering encouragement of my mother and father. Thank you for always believing in me. To my editors, Meredith Norwich, Bethany Nelson, and the entire team at Routledge, thank you for believing in this project and for your expert guidance in shepherding it from a manuscript into the final book you see today.

My professional journey has been shaped by incredible mentors. I would like to particularly thank Young Sohn, Dong Su Kim, and Dmitry Grishin. You each provided me with a platform, encouraged me to build and test new theses, mentor founders, and test the boundaries with thought leadership in publications and speaking at events. This book is a direct result of the opportunities you afforded me.

This book’s technical accuracy was sharpened by the insights of many. My thanks to Melissa Klaerner, whose legal experience provided an invaluable sanity check on the rare and damaging terms that I (thankfully) never saw in person. I am also deeply grateful to the many founders and fellow CVCs who could speak to me only under the condition of anonymity. You know who you are, and I appreciate your commitment to helping the next generation, even when you cannot be named.

Finally, to all the founders in the trenches, building the future: this book is for you.

Disclaimers

Representations: The views expressed in this book are solely that of Freddy Dopfel and do not represent that of any current or previous employer.

Legal: This book is not legal advice. Seek a legal counsel before signing any document. This book should be used in preparation of discussions with a lawyer, not in substitution of them. Examples in this book are purely fictional. Any similarities to real events should be treated as coincidence.

AI Tools: This book was created with the assistance of various AI tools to enhance efficiency in specific tasks, while ensuring that all core content originates from human expertise and creativity. Web research was assisted by Google Search AI Overview, Google Gemini 2.5 Pro, Google Gemini Deep Research, ChatGPT 5.1 Thinking, Perplexity Pro, and Grok 4 Expert, then validated by human experts in the field. Superhuman AI Assistant, Notion AI, and Fathom were used to transcribe, search, cross-reference, and synthesize research from interviews, notes, and email correspondence. Outlines and early drafts were typed by hand or transcribed with Siri or Wispr Flow. Language was adjusted for consistency and style by Grammarly, Google Gemini 2.5 Pro, and Microsoft Word Spellcheck. Final drafts were edited by hand. The ideas, format, words, and authorship remain the work of myself, a human being.

About the Author

Freddy Dopfel is a venture capitalist, engineer, and thought leader focused on the intersection of innovation and entrepreneurship. In 2025, he was named "Corporate VC of the Year" by the Association for Corporate Growth. Freddy's commentary on technology, investing, and innovation has appeared in TechCrunch, VentureBeat, and other leading publications. He frequently speaks to founders, MBA programs, and corporate audiences about startup partnerships, emerging technologies, and the evolving role of CVC.

Freddy helps founders translate technical breakthroughs into scalable businesses. His experience includes investor roles at leading CVC (LG Technology Ventures and Samsung Ventures) and institutional venture capital and private equity firms (Grishin Robotics and CPP Investments). He has led investments across artificial intelligence, robotics, deep tech, semiconductors, advanced materials, and digital platforms.

Freddy Dopfel holds an M.S. with focus on Technology & Engineering Management from Stanford University and a B.S. in Engineering Physics from UC Berkeley. He serves as a mentor with Stanford's Lean Launchpad and for multiple incubators and accelerators.

Introduction

Why Does This Book Exist?

Substantial literature exists concerning corporate venture capital (CVC), predominantly focusing on the initiation and management of CVC units by corporations. Academic studies, white papers from consulting firms, and case studies in business journals abound, all meticulously analyzing the CVC phenomenon. However, they almost universally adopt the viewpoint of the corporate parent building its CVC arm, treating the startup as the object of analysis rather than the protagonist of its own story. These resources answer questions for the executive: How should we structure our fund? How do we measure strategic ROI? How can we de-risk our investment? In this narrative, the founder is a variable in the corporation's equation.

Likewise, a wealth of excellent resources is available for startups on pitching to traditional venture capitalists, guiding them through the mechanics of a standard fundraising process, from designing a pitch deck to negotiating a term sheet. However, a significant and perilous gap exists in the guidance available to founders on navigating the specific nuances of engaging with CVC firms, where strategic imperatives and financial logic collide.

This is not just a theoretical gap; it is one I have witnessed repeatedly in practice. As a mentor to numerous startups, I am consistently confronted with the same set of urgent, high-stakes questions on whether and how founders should work with CVC firms.

This gap in founder-focused literature is mirrored in academia. I recall my own graduate studies at Stanford, where the venture capital curriculum was, quite rightly, steeped in the institutional General Partner/Limited Partner (GP/LP) model. The specific, complex, and often-conflicting world of corporate venture was largely a footnote. This is, in part, because the market itself has transformed so dramatically since venture capital-focused curricula were first developed. CVC has evolved from a niche activity into a meaningful participant, with corporate investors now participating in

DOI: 10.4324/9781003758280-1

over a fifth of all venture deals. The playbook of the past is simply no longer sufficient for the market of today.

This is a critical oversight, given the immense and growing scale of CVC activity. According to Pitchbook, CVC groups participated in deals worth over $120 billion globally[1] in 2024 alone. According to data from the venture-specialist law firm Foley & Lardner, a remarkable 21% of all VC deals in the decade from 2014 to 2024 featured at least one CVC investor.[2] CVC is no longer a niche corner of the venture landscape; it is a mainstream force that founders must be prepared to negotiate with.

This guide aims to address this deficit, providing founders already acquainted with institutional venture capital fundraising with the specialized knowledge necessary to navigate the complexities of corporate venture deals. The core challenge, and the reason this book is necessary, lies in the CVC's inherent dual mandate: the simultaneous pursuit of strategic objectives for the parent corporation and financial returns for the fund. This duality creates a unique set of opportunities and risks that are fundamentally different from those in a traditional VC partnership.

Navigating this landscape requires a multifaceted perspective, as the motivations and consequences of a CVC's actions can appear completely different depending on where one sits at the table. The insights in this guide are drawn from direct experience across this venture ecosystem: mentoring founders through the complexities of CVC negotiations; working from within different corporate venture units, observing their internal pressures and varied operational models; and sitting on the other side of the table in institutional funds, providing an unfiltered view of how CVCs are perceived as co-investors. It is this composite view that allows this book to translate the corporate mindset for the entrepreneur.

It is highly recommended that founders who lack familiarity with general fundraising procedures first consult "Venture Deals" by Brad Feld and Jason Mendelson or the plethora of online resources that discuss the fundraising process in depth. Existing work lays a comprehensive foundation for understanding term sheets and negotiations with institutional VCs. Where "Venture Deals" and books like it are an overview course for venture capital, this guide should be considered a necessary companion, building upon that foundational knowledge and delving into the intricacies of corporate ventures from a perspective that appreciates all sides of the transaction.

What You Will Learn

In this guide, founders will gain insights into the following critical areas:

- **Strategic Assessment of CVC Partnerships**: You will find a framework for evaluating the profound pros and cons of partnering with CVC.

You will learn to determine whether the allure of a strategic partnership aligns with your startup's long-term objectives or if it presents an unacceptable risk to your autonomy and vision.

- **Preparation for CVC Engagement**: You will learn strategies for effectively preparing for pitches and meetings with CVC firms, with a particular focus on how to frame your company's narrative to appeal to both strategic and financial motivations, and crucially, what sensitive information to share and when.
- **Inquiry Strategies for CVC Due Diligence**: This guide will arm you with the essential questions to ask CVCs to dissect their motivations, operational structures, and potential impact on your startup. You will discover how to identify the "gold standard" CVCs and recognize the red flags of potentially problematic partners.
- **CVC-Specific Deal Terms**: A deep dive into the unique deal terms, particularly those found in side letters, that are frequently encountered in CVC transactions. You will gain the ability to understand and effectively negotiate these complex provisions.
- **Balancing Corporate and Startup Interests**: You will learn to master the delicate art of reconciling the project demands and strategic objectives of a CVC partner with the core mission of building an independent, scalable venture, ensuring you can leverage the corporate relationship while protecting your company and its intellectual property.

What You Will Not Learn

This guide assumes a baseline understanding of traditional venture capital processes and is intentionally focused. Consequently, the following topics will not be extensively covered:

- **Fundamentals of Term Sheet Negotiation**: Detailed discussions of standard term sheet clauses like liquidation preferences or anti-dilution, which are thoroughly covered in existing venture capital texts and online resources.
- **General Board Meeting Dynamics and Management**: Procedures and best practices for conducting board meetings, which are applicable across all investor types. This book instead focuses on tactics for avoiding corporate influence in your governance.
- **Basic Pitch Deck Creation**: The fundamentals of crafting a general pitch deck for fundraising. This book instead focuses on how to tailor your pitch specifically for a CVC audience.
- **Legal Counsel**: This book is a strategic guide intended to illuminate the business context and commercial implications of CVC deal terms. **THIS BOOK IS NOT, AND SHOULD NOT BE CONSIDERED, LEGAL**

ADVICE. The goal is to arm you with the right questions and context to have a more effective engagement with potential investors and your own legal counsel as you negotiate the binding terms of an investment and partnership.

Notes

1 PitchBook Data, Inc., and National Venture Capital Association, *Q3 2025 PitchBook–NVCA Venture Monitor*, 2025, https://nvca.org/wp-content/uploads/2025/10/Q3-2025-PitchBook-NVCA-Venture-Monitor.pdf.

2 Louis Lehot, "Where Is Corporate Venture Capital Headed in 2025, and Will It Lead to More M&A?" *Foley Ignite* (Foley & Lardner LLP), February 11, 2025, https://www.foley.com/insights/publications/2025/02/corporate-venture-capital-2025-more-m-a/.

Chapter 1

Strategic Ally or "Dumb Money"

Why Should You Work with a CVC?

A specter haunts the venture capital landscape, or so some would have you believe. Among a segment of traditional, top-tier institutional venture capital (VC) firms, a persistent narrative casts Corporate Venture Capital (CVC) as "dumb money." The assertion, often whispered in Sand Hill Road cafes or stated more bluntly in closed-door partner meetings, is that CVCs, by their very nature, "have no business in venture capital." Fred Wilson of Union Square Ventures famously called CVCs "The Devil" and publicly stated "I hate corporate investment. Corporate investment is dumb."[1] This skepticism is primarily rooted in the perceived inherent conflict arising from the dual mandate most CVCs operate under: the pursuit of both strategic alignment with the parent corporation and financial returns for their fund. Can a CVC truly serve two masters? And more importantly, what does this mean for the ambitious startup founder weighing their funding options?

The critique often centers on the idea that strategic objectives will inevitably trump sound financial decision-making, leading CVCs to make sub-optimal investment choices, overpay, or impose onerous terms that benefit the parent company at the startup's expense. Esteemed startup accelerators like YCombinator have historically advised their cohorts to be wary, specifically cautioning against granting CVCs board or even board observer seats, fearing that the corporate parent's agenda could unduly influence or stifle a nascent company's trajectory.

While these concerns are not without historical precedent and warrant careful consideration, the narrative of CVCs as universally "dumb money" is an oversimplification that risks blinding founders to a potent source of value. The landscape of corporate venturing has matured significantly. Many CVCs are now run by seasoned investment professionals with considerable autonomy and a clear understanding that the best strategic returns often flow from financially successful, independent companies. At the same time, new CVCs are forming every month, and many may

DOI: 10.4324/9781003758280-2

operate without the expertise of a seasoned VC team, focusing primarily on reporting to headquarters.

The question, then, is not just why a corporate VC would want to invest in your startup, but the far more critical one for you, the founder: **Why should your startup want to work with a corporate VC?**

In a competitive funding environment, every venture capital firm, institutional or corporate, strives to differentiate itself. They broadcast their value-add, hoping to secure an allocation in promising deals. Some funds highlight their expansive networks for customer introductions; others tout deep sector expertise or offer operational support in areas like marketing, talent acquisition, and HR to help sculpt a company from its earliest days.

Corporate VCs are no different in their need to demonstrate value beyond the capital they provide. However, the *nature* of their value proposition can be uniquely powerful. Quite to the contrary of claims of "dumb money," there actually exists a measurable "CVC Alpha." A substantial body of evidence demonstrates that CVC-backed startups outperform their Institutional VC-backed peers across several critical metrics. According to research by Global Corporate Venturing and Pitchbook, startups backed by CVCs have a substantially lower risk of bankruptcy and greater valuation multiples.[2] McKinsey research shows that startups with a CVC backer in their first three financing rounds have a 21–64% higher chance of a successful exit and are more likely to stay in business.[3]

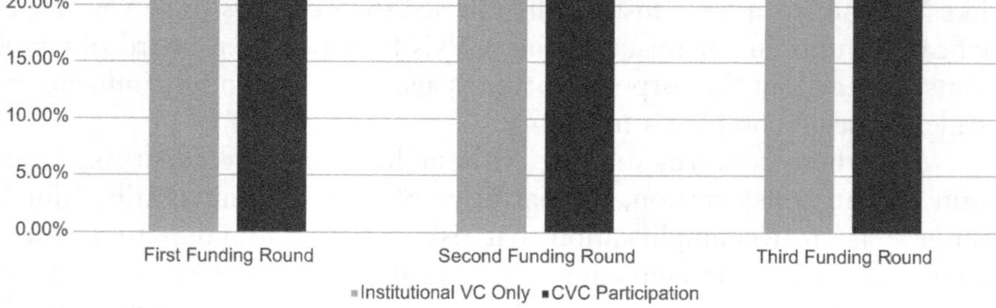

Exhibit 1.1 Startup exits via IPO/M&A/LBO by 7th round of financing (higher is better) according to McKinsey "How to make investments in start-ups pay off," 2022.

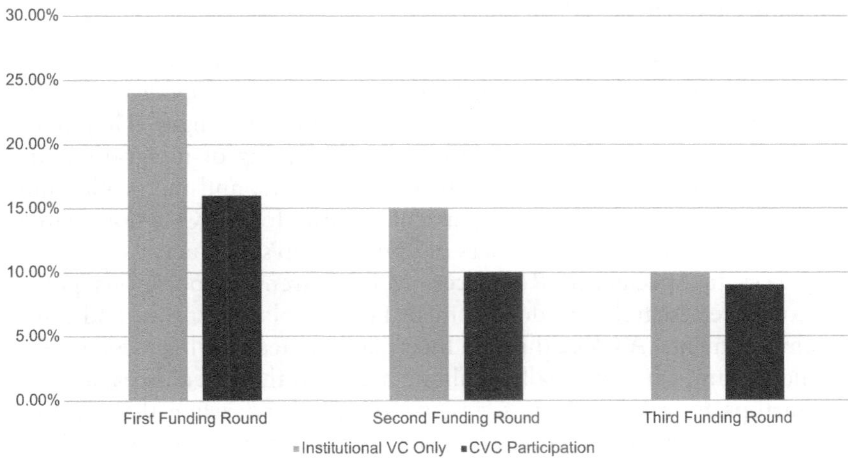

Exhibit 1.2 Startups out of business by 7th funding round (lower is better) according to McKinsey "How to make investments in start-ups pay off," 2022.

Are CVCs, despite their requirements to focus on startups within narrow strategic scopes, better at "picking winners" than their institutional counterparts? I believe not! This outperformance comes from the unique value that a CVC can bring to their portfolio companies. Beyond the check, CVCs primarily offer three major non-monetary advantages that can be transformative for a startup:

1 Deep Industry Expertise and Validation
2 Strategic Corporate Development and Customer Access
3 Powerful Market Signaling and Credibility

Let us dissect each of these to understand their tangible impact.

Deep Industry Expertise and Validation: Beyond Surface-Level Knowledge

By their very definition, CVCs are extensions of corporations that are often leaders or significant players within specific industries. This lineage provides them with an ingrained, nuanced understanding of the field in which their parent company operates: an understanding that typically runs far deeper than that of a generalist VC. They live and breathe the market dynamics, competitive pressures, technological shifts, and regulatory intricacies of their sector.

Tangible Benefits for a Startup

- **Informed Strategic Guidance**: A CVC with genuine domain expertise can offer invaluable advice on product-market fit, competitive positioning, and navigating complex industry-specific challenges. They understand the legacy systems you might be disrupting or integrating with, the entrenched behaviors of potential customers, and the subtle unmet needs of the market. This is particularly true for CVCs whose parents are likely to be large customers of your startup's product.
- **Access to Specialized Resources**: Many parent corporations possess extensive research and development facilities, laboratories, and testing environments. A CVC, through their platform team or business development team, can potentially facilitate access to these resources, allowing startups to validate claims, test prototypes, and refine their technology with a rigor that might otherwise be unattainable or prohibitively expensive. Imagine a biotech startup gaining access to a pharmaceutical giant's advanced screening tools or a materials science company utilizing a CVC parent's specialized testing equipment.
- **Market Ecosystem Intelligence**: Corporates often have a panoramic view of their industry's ecosystem, having invested in, partnered with, or competed against a multitude of players. This perspective allows them to provide startups with critical insights into market trends, emerging threats, and potential partnership opportunities that might not be visible from the outside.
- **Leveraged Diligence for Future Rounds**: The technical and market diligence performed by a reputable CVC is often highly regarded by institutional VCs. Even if the CVC is not leading the investment round, their participation can act as a powerful validation. Institutional VCs, particularly those who are generalists or have less depth in a specific niche, will often leverage the CVC's technical due diligence as a crucial part of their own decision-making process. This can manifest as sharing data from laboratory tests, pilot programs, or detailed market analyses conducted by the CVC's internal experts. This "borrowed conviction" can significantly de-risk the investment for other VCs and expedite their process.

In many deals, the presence of a CVC that has thoroughly vetted the technology and market opportunity provides a level of comfort and validation that accelerates the entire fundraising process. Their expertise becomes a de facto seal of approval, signaling that the startup has cleared a high bar for technical and commercial viability within that specific industry. I have been part of multiple deep tech deals where institutional investors would base their investment decision on whether the CVC would join or not because of the deep diligence the CVC performs.

Strategic Corporate Development and Customer Access: Opening Doors from Within

One of the most tantalizing prospects of partnering with a CVC is the potential access to the parent corporation as a major customer, strategic partner, or distribution channel. While it's crucial for founders to understand that a CVC investment rarely comes with a guaranteed commercial contract, it can undeniably open influential doors and create powerful internal advocates that help build that contract down the road.

Navigating the Path to Partnership

- **The Internal Champion**: CVCs, while typically maintaining a degree of separation from the parent company's procurement divisions, can act as powerful internal champions for their portfolio companies. They understand the corporate labyrinth and can facilitate introductions to the right decision-makers, often at the C-suite level. This top-down advocacy can be a vital complement to a startup's typical bottom-up sales efforts, potentially shortening sales cycles for complex enterprise solutions.
- **Early Customer Insights**: Even if a formal customer agreement isn't immediately forthcoming, the CVC and its parent can provide invaluable, early insights into the needs, expectations, and procurement processes of large corporate customers. This "voice of the customer" feedback can be instrumental in refining a startup's product, go-to-market strategy, and enterprise-readiness, not just for the CVC's parent, but for all potential large customers.
- **Pilot Programs and Proof-of-Concepts (PoCs)**: An investment from a CVC can often pave the way for pilot programs or PoC deployments within the parent organization. These initial engagements are critical for validating a startup's solution in a real-world enterprise environment, generating case studies, and building credibility. A successful pilot with a leading corporation can be a game-changer for attracting further customers and investors.
- **Distribution Channels and Market Access**: Beyond direct sales to the parent, CVCs can sometimes unlock access to the corporation's established distribution channels, partner ecosystems, or international markets. This can provide a startup with a significant unfair advantage in scaling its reach far more rapidly than it could on its own.

It's important for founders to approach this aspect with realistic expectations. The CVC's role is often that of a facilitator and advocate, not a director of the parent company's commercial decisions. However, a CVC whose parent company represents a significant target market for the startup can create a powerful alignment of interests, where the success of the startup directly contributes to the strategic objectives of the corporate investor.

Powerful Market Signaling and Credibility: The Badge of Validation

Even if renowned investment firms YCombinator, Sequoia Capital, and Andreessen Horowitz (a16z) offered no tangible value-add services beyond their capital, founders would still clamor for their investment. Why? Because the association itself, the "signaling effect," is immensely powerful. An investment from a highly respected firm bestows a badge of credibility that resonates throughout the market. This is not merely about "bragging rights." It has profound implications for attracting top talent, securing subsequent funding rounds, and building market trust. Corporate VCs, particularly those associated with well-respected industry leaders, can offer a similar, potent signaling effect, often with a specialized flavor.

The Value of Association

- **Sector-Specific Validation**: An investment from the CVC arm of a recognized leader in your industry sends a clear message: your startup's technology, team, and vision have been vetted and validated by experts who truly understand the domain. Consider an encryption startup: securing an investment from In-Q-Tel (the strategic investment arm of the U.S. Intelligence Community) is a monumental signal. It implies that the technology has passed incredibly rigorous technical diligence and that the company is, at the very least, in substantive discussions with a potentially massive and influential customer base (the Department of War and other government agencies). In-Q-Tel's involvement signals not only financial backing but also deep technical validation and a pathway to critical government markets.
- **De-risking for Follow-On Investors**: Venture capital is often characterized by a "herd mentality." While this is a somewhat cynical view, it contains a kernel of truth. VCs operate under time constraints and information asymmetry. They look for credible signals of traction, competence, and market validation to help them prioritize opportunities and confirm their own assumptions before committing to deep diligence. Imagine a generalist VC encounters a promising but highly technical semiconductor chip-design company. The VC might be intrigued but hesitant, perhaps questioning the market timing or the true scale of the problem, especially as they have not previously done extensive background research in the semiconductor space. If they

then discover that Intel Capital, Samsung Ventures, or TSMC directly is already an investor, or better yet, investing in this current round, their perception can shift dramatically. The implicit question becomes: "If these global leaders in chip design and fabrication are sufficiently excited to invest, what critical insights am I missing? What do they know that I don't? Shouldn't I take a deeper look?" The CVC's presence acts as a powerful validator, prompting other investors to overcome initial skepticism.
- **Attracting Talent and Partnerships**: The credibility conferred by a strategic CVC investor can also make it easier to attract top-tier talent. Engineers, scientists, and business leaders are often more willing to join a startup that is backed and validated by a major player in their field. Similarly, other potential strategic partners may be more inclined to engage with a startup that can show off the logo of a respected corporate investor.

The Strategic Role of CVCs: More Than Just a Check

It is important to note that CVCs do not always need to be, and often should not be, the largest check in any given funding round. Their most profound value to a startup is frequently non-monetary. Their expertise is in bringing strategic value to a startup, not finding the optimal price for a fundraising round. They can serve as crucial strategic co-investors, bringing industry-specific expertise, customer access, and market credibility that complements the financial discipline and broader network of institutional VCs.

The decision to take CVC funding is a strategic one that requires careful due diligence by the founder. Understanding the CVC's mandate, their track record, the level of autonomy they have from the parent company, and the specific strategic value they can bring is paramount. But to dismiss all CVCs as "dumb money" is to potentially overlook a powerful ally that can provide critical, non-dilutive advantages on the challenging journey of building a successful company. The smart founder will look beyond the label and assess the unique strategic leverage a CVC can offer.

Notes

1 CB Insights, "Fred Wilson Hates Corporate VCs, Talks Dumb Money and Blockchain," *Medium*, July 18, 2016, https://medium.com/@CBinsights/fred-wilson-hates-corporate-vcs-talks-dumb-money-and-blockchain-a028448bb8c4
2 Maija Palmer, "Corporate-Backed Startups Are More Likely to Survive," *Global Corporate Venturing*, August 4, 2023, https://globalventuring.com/corporate/corporate-backed-startups-are-more-likely-to-survive/

3 Matt Banholzer, John Levene, and Sid Ramtri, "How to Make Investments in Start-ups Pay Off," *McKinsey & Company*, November 9, 2022, https://www.mckinsey.com/capabilities/strategy-and-corporate-finance/our-insights/how-to-make-investments-in-start-ups-pay-off

Chapter 2

CVC Structures and Motivations (And Why They Matter to You)

While the world of institutional venture capital largely adheres to a standardized playbook, the General Partner/Limited Partner (GP/LP) model, the corporate venture capital (CVC) landscape presents a far more varied terrain. CVC firms are not monolithic: they come in a diverse array of shapes and sizes, each with its own structural nuances and underlying motivations. For a startup founder, understanding these differences is not merely an academic exercise; it's a critical piece of due diligence that can dramatically influence the nature of the relationship, the alignment of interests, and ultimately, the success of the partnership.

To navigate this complex ecosystem, it's essential to first grasp the benchmark: the traditional institutional VC structure.

The Institutional VC Blueprint: A Primer on the GP/LP Model

Multiple literary and online sources dive deep into an exhaustive exploration of the intricacies of venture capital deal structures. However, for our purposes, a concise overview of the dominant GP/LP model will suffice.

A typical institutional VC fund is defined by:

- **Limited Partners (LPs)**: These are the primary investors *in* the venture capital fund. LPs are typically large institutions such as pension funds, university endowments, foundations, family offices, or high-net-worth individuals. They commit capital to the fund for a defined period (often ten years, with potential extensions) with the expectation of receiving significant returns on their investment. LPs generally take a passive role, providing capital but not being involved in the fund's day-to-day investment decisions.
- **General Partners (GPs)**: These are the individuals who manage the venture capital fund. They are the active decision-makers responsible for sourcing deal flow, conducting due diligence, making investment

DOI: 10.4324/9781003758280-3

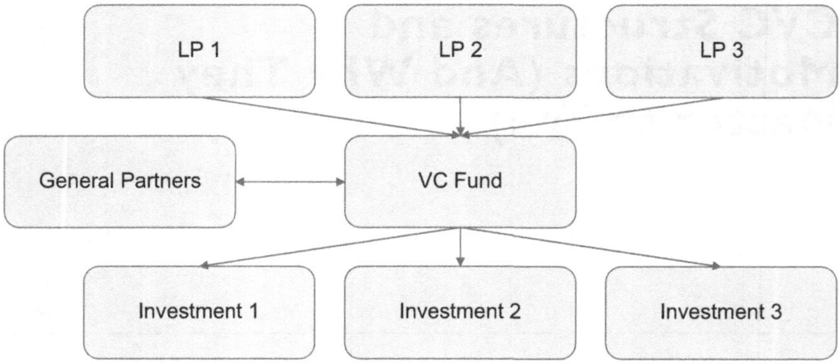

Exhibit 2.1 A diagram showcasing the structure of a traditional GP/LP structure as seen in institutional venture capital.

decisions, sitting on portfolio company boards, and working to help their portfolio companies succeed. The GP entity (often a management company) raises capital from LPs to form the fund. "General Partner" is also often a job title, and in most institutional funds, the GPs alone are the decision-makers in an investment committee (although Principals, Associates, and Analysts are non-voting voices and potential advocates).

- **Fund Economics**: GPs are typically compensated through two primary mechanisms:
  - **Management Fees**: An annual fee (commonly 2%) charged on the total committed capital of the fund. This fee covers the operational expenses of the VC firm, including employee salary and office rent.
  - **Carried Interest (Carry)**: A share (typically 20%) of the fund's profits *after* the LPs have received their initial investment back (and often a preferred return, or "hurdle rate"). This is the primary incentive for GPs to generate strong financial returns. It is effectively the "performance bonus" of VC fund employees, but is only paid out many years after a successful investment, when the company has an exit.

This GP/LP structure creates a clear fiduciary duty for the GPs to maximize financial returns for their LPs. While value-add services are crucial for attracting top startups, the ultimate yardstick of success for an institutional VC is the financial performance of its fund. For an institutional VC, value-added services are a means to the end goal of financial return. For a CVC firm, strategic alignment often *is* the end goal.

The CVC Spectrum: Beyond a One-Size-Fits-All Approach

CVC units diverge significantly from this standardized institutional model. Their structures are often tailored to the specific objectives and constraints of their parent corporation. While numerous permutations exist, CVCs generally vary along three primary axes: **Fund Structure, Investment Motivation**, and **Legal Structure**. Understanding where a particular CVC falls on these axes is paramount for any founder considering their investment, as it can affect the motivation of the CVC and where and how your interests are aligned with theirs.

Fund Structure: Where Does the Money Come From?

The way a CVC's capital is sourced and managed directly impacts its investment horizon, risk appetite, and decision-making processes.

- **The GP/LP Structure** (**The "Institutionalized" CVC**): Some CVCs adopt a structure that mirrors traditional VCs. In this model, the parent corporation acts as a significant, and often sole, LP in a fund managed by a dedicated team of investment professionals (the GPs). This structure can provide the CVC with greater autonomy and a clearer focus on financial returns, as the fund managers are often incentivized with carried interest or "phantom carry" (bonuses meant to imitate the value of carried interest), similar to their institutional counterparts. This is often the most preferred structure from a startup's perspective as it aligns incentives more closely with financial success and can offer more predictable investment behavior. These CVCs may also raise capital from external LPs alongside the parent corporation, further institutionalizing their approach.
    - **Implications for Startups**: From a founder's perspective, the GP/LP structure is often the most desirable CVC model as it most closely mirrors the operations and incentives of a traditional institutional fund. The presence of carried interest or phantom carry strongly aligns the CVC's goals with the startup's: achieving the highest possible financial exit. This structure often leads to more predictable and professional behavior, as the CVC team typically has a streamlined, institutional-style due diligence and investment committee process. Furthermore, the committed capital of a dedicated fund provides stability, insulating the CVC from the parent's quarterly budget shifts and increasing the reliability of follow-on funding.

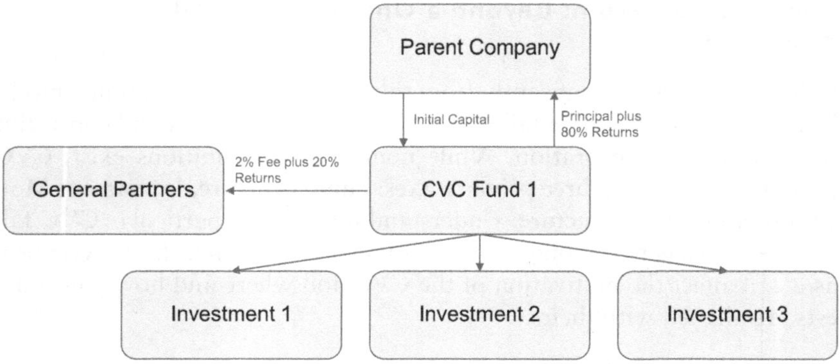

Exhibit 2.2 A diagram showcasing the structure of a CVC employing a GP/LP structure.

- **Balance Sheet Investing (Direct Corporate Allocation)**: This is the most common CVC model. Here, investments are made directly from the parent corporation's balance sheet. There isn't a formally committed "fund" in the traditional sense. Instead, capital is allocated on a deal-by-deal basis. The Global Corporate Venturing (GCV) organization estimates that 74% of CVCs invest off balance sheet.[1]
  - **Implications for Startups**: This structure can lead to more variability in investment pacing and decision-making. Investment approvals might be subject to the parent company's current financial performance, shifting strategic priorities, or internal budgetary cycles. While potentially offering access to significant capital, the process can sometimes be slower or more bureaucratic, involving multiple layers of corporate approval. However, it can also mean that if a startup is highly strategic to the parent, larger sums of capital might be deployed more flexibly than from a fixed-size fund, which has constraints on minimum and maximum check size.

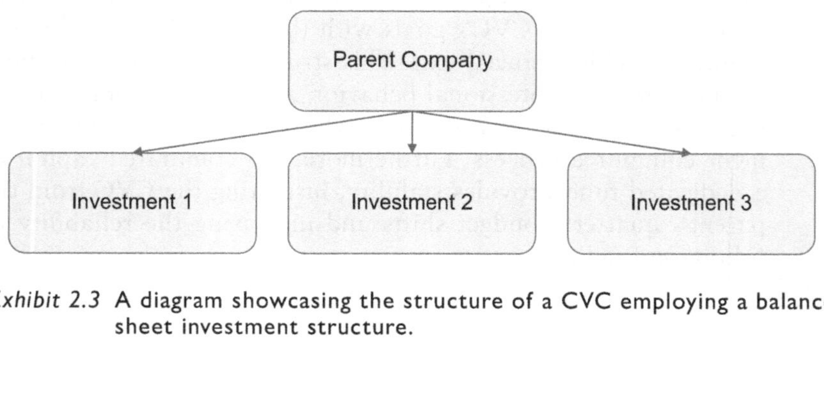

Exhibit 2.3 A diagram showcasing the structure of a CVC employing a balance sheet investment structure.

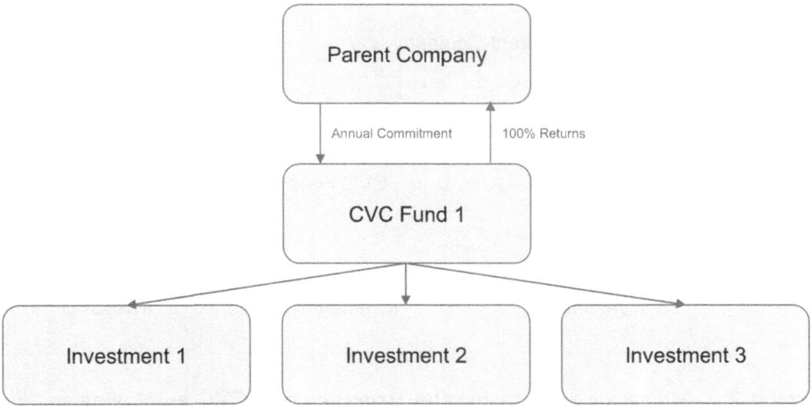

Exhibit 2.4 A diagram showcasing the structure of a CVC employing an "Evergreen" continuous capital replenishment structure.

- **Evergreen Funds (Continuous Capital Replenishment/Annual Commitment)**: An evergreen fund is a variation of balance sheet investing where the CVC has a dedicated pool of capital that is replenished by the parent corporation, often on an annual basis. This model aims to provide a more consistent and long-term source of investment capital, mitigating some of the cyclicality that can affect pure balance sheet investing.
    - **Implications for Startups**: Evergreen funds can signal a more sustained commitment to venture investing by the parent corporation than traditional balance sheet investing. They often strike a balance, offering more stability than ad-hoc balance sheet investing while still being closely tied to the parent's strategic interests. The key for founders is to understand how regularly and reliably the fund is replenished. Renewing evergreen funds is usually a "handshake agreement" rather than a legal obligation, so although it is less susceptible to budget shifts than a direct balance sheet investing CVC, extreme unforeseen budget concerns or business strategy shifts may still jeopardize them.
- **Evergreen Funds (Recycling Fund Returns)**: This is a more sophisticated and far more powerful evergreen structure. In this model, the proceeds from successful exits (i.e., the cash returned when a portfolio company is acquired or goes public) are not returned to the parent corporation's treasury. Instead, they are "recycled" directly back into the CVC's fund, becoming new capital available for future investments.
    - **Implications for Startups**: The recycling model is one of the strongest positive signals a founder can encounter. It indicates a high level of

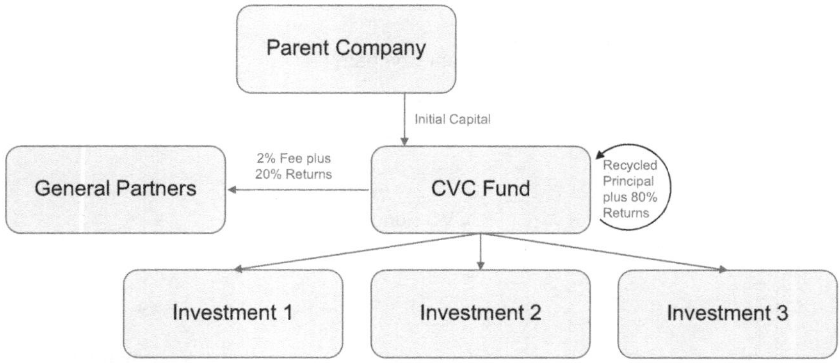

Exhibit 2.5 **A diagram showcasing the structure of a CVC employing an "Evergreen" recycled returns structure.**

trust and long-term commitment from the parent company, who has empowered the CVC to become at least partially self-sustaining. This structure creates a virtuous cycle: the CVC is intensely motivated to help its portfolio companies achieve strong financial exits, because that success directly fuels its ability to make new investments and continue its operations. It insulates the CVC from the whims of corporate budget cycles and aligns their incentives much more closely with those of a traditional, financially driven institutional GP/LP fund. However, limited "dry powder" can be a risk if the fund has deployed too quickly and not realized exits.

Investment Motivation: The Strategic Versus Financial Spectrum

A pivotal question every founder should explore when engaging with a CVC is: "Are your investment decisions primarily driven by strategic objectives or financial returns?" The reality is that most CVCs operate somewhere on a spectrum between these two poles. Few are *purely* strategic (indifferent to financial loss) or *purely* financial (with no regard for strategic relevance to the parent). The specific balance a CVC strikes is often a result of internal negotiations and the relative influence of different corporate functions. When a CVC is formed, it must typically satisfy the needs of multiple masters from its corporate parent: the Chief Financial Officer (CFO), who is primarily concerned with return on investment; the Chief Executive Officer (CEO), who is focused on how new technologies can be implemented to drive the core business; and the Chief Strategy Officer (CSO) or Chief Technology Officer (CTO), who is interested in the long-term strategic implications of market shifts and disruptive innovations. The resulting investment motivation is often a blend of these competing priorities.

Primarily Strategic CVCs

At the far strategic end of the spectrum, these CVC units invest almost exclusively to support the goals of the parent corporation. Their mission is not to generate venture-grade returns, but to serve as a strategic weapon. This could involve acting as a "window on technology" to gain early insights into emerging trends, functioning as an external R&D arm to access potential acquisition targets, fostering an ecosystem of companies that build on the parent's platform, or even making defensive investments to block competitors from gaining a technological edge. For these CVCs, financial returns, while welcome, are a secondary concern to the strategic value delivered back to the parent. After all, if the parent company is selling tens of billions of dollars of widgets a year, what do they care about a $10 million investment return?

- **Potential Upsides for Startups**: A CVC with a purely strategic mandate can be a powerful ally if your startup is of high importance to the parent. They may be valuation-insensitive, or significantly more flexible on valuation and terms, as their decision is not constrained by traditional financial return hurdles. These CVCs can also offer the deepest level of integration with the parent company, providing unparalleled access to resources, market channels, and internal expertise. They are often highly motivated to see a commercial partnership succeed, as this is the primary metric by which their own performance is judged.
- **Potential Downsides for Startups**: The dreaded "dumb money" label is most often, and sometimes fairly, applied here. A lack of financial discipline can lead to irrational behavior. More importantly, the CVC's priorities are unequivocally tied to the parent's agenda, which may not align with your startup's optimal path to independent success. This can manifest as pressure for exclusive partnerships that limit your market, premature acquisition discussions at a suboptimal price, or a demand to focus on features that benefit the parent rather than the broader market you need to capture.
    - **The Tech Scouting Trap**: A significant, related risk is that a CVC focused on strategic intelligence may be more interested in information gathering for headquarters than in actually making investments. This can lead to a series of promising but ultimately fruitless meetings,

where the startup expends significant time and resources educating the corporate team with no real intention of a deal ever materializing. The CVC isn't aiming to waste your time, and oftentimes CVC employees genuinely believe that their extensive education and diligence can lead to an investment. However, their incentives are to learn, not to make a deal.

  - **The "Endless Diligence" Trap**: This often manifests as a perpetual due diligence process. The CVC team may continually ask for "just one more meeting" with another internal expert, or "a bit more data" for an internal report, without ever moving toward a term sheet or a clear decision.
  - **Free Consulting**: In this dynamic, the startup is effectively providing free consulting and market research to the parent corporation, educating them on emerging technologies and competitive landscapes at the cost of the founder's most valuable asset: their time.
  - **Mitigation**: Founders can mitigate this by performing the diligence on their potential CVC partner outlined in our later chapter on research, preparation, and the key questions to ask to assess this risk early in the process. Probing their investment cadence and decision-making process can help reveal whether they are serious investors or simply information gatherers.

- **The "Strategic Orphan" Risk**: The risk of becoming a "strategic orphan" is acute. If the parent corporation's strategy shifts, either due to a new CEO, a market downturn, or a change in priorities, a startup that was once a perfect strategic fit can suddenly become irrelevant. In such cases, the CVC's support can evaporate overnight, leaving the startup in a precarious position with an investor who is no longer an advocate.
- **Adverse Selection of Talent**: Few accomplished venture capitalists choose to build their careers at a fund with little or no financial incentive. As a result, startups may face an adverse selection bias, working with a team that may lack the experience and network of a seasoned institutional investor.

Primarily Financial CVCs

At the other end of the motivational spectrum are the CVCs that operate with a clear and primary mandate to generate strong financial returns. These organizations function much like their institutional VC counterparts on Sand Hill Road. For them, strategic alignment with the parent corporation is not the core driver of an investment decision; rather, it is a "nice-to-have," or a potential bonus or a factor in tie-breaking decisions between two otherwise equally attractive opportunities. It is an "unfair advantage" both for accessing deals and for helping their investments grow.

Primarily financially oriented CVCs are often granted significant autonomy from the parent company and are typically staffed by professionals with traditional venture capital backgrounds who are compensated based on the financial performance of the fund. Their primary fiduciary duty is to generate a return on the capital invested, which fundamentally shapes their behavior and their relationship with their portfolio companies.

- **Potential Upsides for Startups**
  - **Deeply Aligned Incentives for Value Maximization**: The most significant advantage of partnering with a financially driven CVC is the clean alignment of incentives. Their primary goal is the same as yours and that of your institutional investors: to maximize the standalone value of your company to achieve the best possible exit. This means they will be supportive of decisions that drive enterprise value, whether that's pursuing a large new market that is irrelevant to the parent company or accepting an acquisition offer from a third party (even a competitor to their parent) if it represents the best outcome for shareholders. This alignment removes the potential for conflict when a startup's optimal path diverges from the parent corporation's strategic interests.
  - **Rational and Financially Disciplined Decision-Making**: Because their success is measured by financial metrics like internal rate of return (IRR) and cash-on-cash return, these CVCs tend to make decisions that are rational, predictable, and disciplined. They are less likely to be swayed by internal corporate politics or a sudden shift in the parent company's strategy. This predictability is especially valuable when it comes to follow-on funding. A financially driven CVC will typically assess a subsequent round based on the startup's progress and market traction, much like any other institutional investor, rather than on whether a specific strategic milestone for the parent has been met.
  - **Easier Syndicate Building**: Institutional VCs are often more comfortable co-investing alongside a financially driven CVC. They understand their motivations and can be confident that the CVC will behave as a rational financial actor at the board level and during exit negotiations. Notably, financially driven CVCs are usually fine with co-investing with CVCs from their parents' competitors. This can make it significantly easier to build a strong, cohesive investor syndicate.

- **Potential Downsides for Startups**
    - **The "Value-Add" Gap**: The most obvious downside is that a CVC focused purely on financial returns may offer less direct strategic assistance or deep integration with the parent company. The introductions to key business units, access to specialized R&D facilities, or facilitation of pilot programs may be less forthcoming. While they carry the corporate parent's name, they may not have the internal incentives or dedicated resources to actively build the bridge between the startup and the corporate behemoth. The "corporate" benefits can become more passive than active. They are motivated to help because it can have long-term value-add to their investment, but building alignment has less of an impact on their next bonus or quarterly key performance indicator (KPI).
    - **The Signaling Paradox: The Investor Who Isn't a Customer**: This is a subtle but significant risk. If you have a major, globally recognized corporation in your industry on your cap table, but they are *not* a customer, it can create a negative signal in the market. Other potential investors and, more importantly, other potential customers may ask a very pointed question: "If your technology is so compelling, why isn't your investor's parent company using it?" It can create the perception that the parent corporation "looked under the hood and didn't like what they saw," even if the reality is simply that the CVC operates with a strict separation. Although nobody would expect them to become an immediate customer, especially if you are an early-stage startup, this can become a recurring and difficult question to answer in future fundraising and sales efforts, forcing the founder to constantly explain the nuances of their investor's operating model.
    - **Potentially Less Patience**: In some cases, a purely financial CVC might be less patient with a struggling portfolio company than a strategic one. If a startup is failing to meet its financial projections, a financial CVC may be quicker to write down the investment and focus its attention elsewhere. A strategic CVC, by contrast, might continue to support the company if it is still providing valuable market intelligence or technology insights to the parent, giving the startup a longer runway to find its footing.

Hybrid CVCs (The Common Ground)

The vast majority of CVCs fall into this category, seeking a balance between strategic impact and financial return. They aim to invest in companies that are not only financially promising but also have some relevance to the parent corporation's current or future business. The weighting between "strategic" and "financial" can vary significantly even within this hybrid category, and understanding this balance is key for any founder. Some hybrid CVCs may have separate teams dedicated to financial investment versus strategic business development, creating a more structured approach to delivering both types of value.

- Examples
  - **Google Ventures** (GV): While part of Alphabet, GV has historically operated with a strong emphasis on financial returns, investing across a broad range of sectors, not all directly tied to Google's core business. Strategic insights are a benefit, but fund performance is key.
  - **Salesforce Ventures**: Clearly invests in companies within the enterprise cloud ecosystem, creating strategic value for Salesforce, but also seeks strong financial outcomes from its portfolio.
  - **BMW iVentures**: Focuses on technologies relevant to the future of mobility, which is highly strategic to BMW, but still operates with the expectation of generating venture-grade financial returns.
  - **LG Technology Ventures**: The VC arm of the LG Group, LG Technology Ventures has a financially driven VC team and has a large business development team dedicated to finding and accelerating strategic alignment of portfolio companies.

Founders should be wary of CVCs that claim to be *entirely* financially driven if they lack the structural autonomy to back it up, or those that are *entirely* strategic, as this can lead to misaligned long-term incentives. The key is to understand the *balance* and how the CVC's internal performance metrics are structured. If a CVC team's compensation is primarily based on strategic milestones for the parent, their behavior will differ from a team compensated on the IRR of their fund.

Legal Structure: Arm's Length or Embedded?

The legal relationship between the CVC unit and its parent corporation has profound implications for information sharing, conflicts of interest, and operational independence.

- **CVC as a Division of the Parent Company**: In this model, the CVC is an internal department, usually sitting within the strategy, R&D, or corporate development (M&A) functions. The CVC team members are employees of the parent corporation.
  - **Implications for Startups**: Information flow between the CVC and the parent is often seamless. This can be beneficial for unlocking

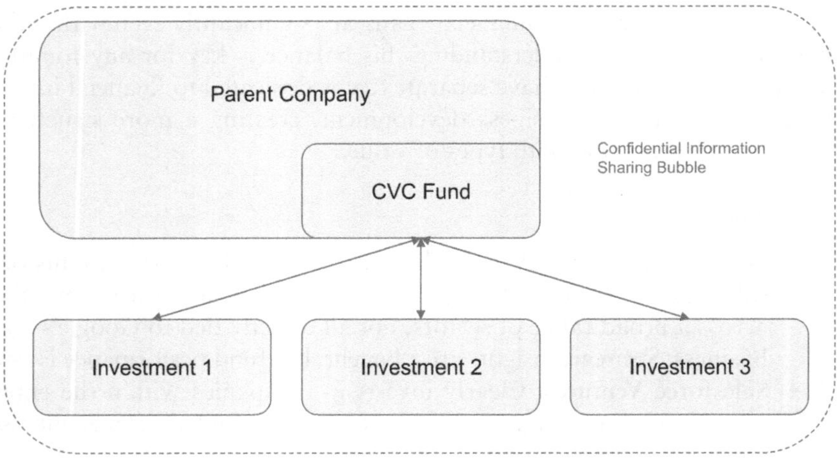

Exhibit 2.6 A diagram showcasing how sensitive information can be shared between startups, the CVC, and the parent company for an integrated CVC fund.

strategic collaborations but also raises concerns about confidentiality. A Non-Disclosure Agreement (NDA) with the CVC might effectively be an NDA with the entire corporation, including potentially competitive business units. This means that information about your revenue, pricing, and other sensitive financial information could travel to the parent company, a potential competitor or customer, and be used against you in negotiation. Decision-making on partnerships can move faster, but decision-making on investment may be more tied-in with corporate rules and bureaucracy.

- **CVC as a Separate Legal Entity**: Here, the CVC is established as a distinct subsidiary, sometimes with its own Board of Directors. While wholly or significantly owned by the parent, it operates with a greater degree of legal and operational separation.
  - **Implications for Startups**: This structure generally offers better protection for a startup's sensitive information. It's possible to have separate NDAs with the CVC entity and parent company, creating a clearer boundary between the investment arm and the parent's operational units. For example, detailed product capabilities and specifics of integration and collaboration may be under NDA with the parent company, but cost structures and financial models may be under a separate NDA with the venture group. This separation can also grant the CVC more autonomy in its investment decisions and make it a more agile partner.

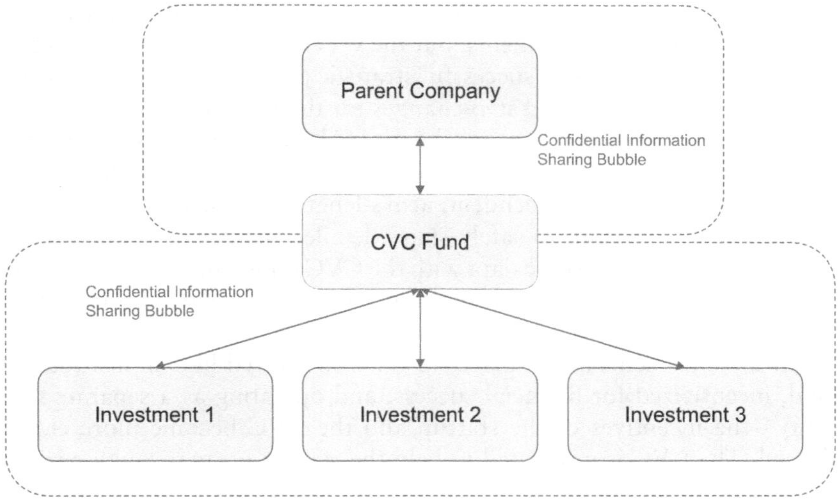

Exhibit 2.7 A diagram showcasing how sensitive information can be shared between startups, the CVC, and the parent company for a legally separate CVC fund.

Regardless of the legal structure of a CVC, it is always best practice to clearly specify which information may be shared with which entities. This is especially true when sending decks and other sensitive information via email. Even small changes like naming documents "Teaser Deck for Widget Ventures.pdf" versus "Teaser Deck for WidgetCorp.pdf" help avoid even accidental oversharing from CVCs to their parent companies.

The "Gold Standard" CVC Profile (From a Startup's Perspective)

While every startup's needs are unique, a CVC structure that often aligns best with a founder's long-term interests typically exhibits the following characteristics:

- **Fund Structure**: A dedicated fund, ideally with a GP/LP-like structure (even if the parent is the sole LP), or a well-capitalized recycling evergreen fund that has been running for some years. This signals a long-term commitment and a degree of financial discipline. The fund is well-incentivized to help your company be a financial success, rather than purely a strategic win for the parent.
- **Investment Motivation**: A hybrid model with a strong, demonstrable emphasis on financial returns, where strategic alignment is a significant plus but not at the expense of the startup's independent success. The

CVC incentives should include a component tied to the financial performance of their investments, but the CVC should also be able to provide ample examples of successful strategic projects with their portfolio companies that provided step-changes for their growth.

- **Legal Structure**: A separate legal entity. This provides maximal protection for the startup's confidential information through distinct NDAs and fosters a more independent, arm's-length relationship. This separation allows a startup to safely share detailed financials, product roadmaps, and other sensitive data with the CVC under an NDA that doesn't automatically expose that information to the entire parent corporation.

When these elements are in place—a CVC structured like an institutional fund, incentivized for financial success, and operating as a separate legal entity—the incentives of the startup and the CVC become more closely aligned. The CVC is motivated to help the startup grow through partnership and achieve a successful exit because that's how *they* achieve their financial targets, which in turn (ideally) delivers strategic value to the parent.

Why This Matters: Concrete Examples of Structural Impact

The seemingly arcane details of a CVC's internal structure are not merely academic; they have profound and lasting consequences for a startup. The following illustrative scenarios demonstrate how, under certain circumstances, the structural model of a CVC partner can dramatically alter a startup's trajectory and ultimate success.

Negative Scenario: The Balance Sheet CVC and the Perils of Corporate Volatility

SunWash, a promising startup in the renewable energy sector that builds robots that automatically clean solar panels, secures an investment from Solar Ventures, the CVC arm of SolarCorp, a major industrial conglomerate that manufactures solar panels. Solar Ventures operates directly off SolarCorp's balance sheet, a common but potentially volatile structure. Initially, the relationship is highly productive, with SunWash gaining valuable industry insights. However, a year into the partnership, SolarCorp faces an unexpected economic downturn and initiates aggressive cost-cutting measures across all "non-core" expenditures.

Solar Ventures, lacking the protection of a dedicated fund, sees its budget immediately slashed. Follow-on funding for SunWash, which was previously all but assured, is put on indefinite hold. Compounding the issue, the SunWash's internal champion at the Solar Ventures, a key advocate for the partnership, is reassigned during the corporate restructuring and the partnership is scrapped. The startup is now in a precarious position. Not only has its strategic partner publicly signaled a loss of confidence by withdrawing from planned collaborations, but the internal team that could explain the situation to new investors has been dismantled. To the outside world, it appears that SunWash's technology has failed to deliver, severely impairing its ability to raise its next round of funding.

Negative Scenario: The Embedded CVC and the Compromise of Intellectual Property

LuminaSense, a seed-stage software startup building an AI engine for real-time anomaly detection in industrial IoT data, accepts a strategic investment from Nebula Ventures, the corporate venture arm of Orion Technologies, a large cloud and semiconductor company. Critically, Nebula Ventures is not a separate legal entity or standalone fund; it is structurally housed inside Orion's Advanced Research Group, with investment staff sitting alongside Orion's applied AI researchers and platform architects. Under the protection of an NDA and in response to detailed technical diligence requests, LuminaSense shares its core design philosophy, model-training pipeline, and high-level microservice architecture with the Nebula team, including how it efficiently processes noisy sensor data at the edge and synchronizes compressed feature representations back to the cloud.

Six months later, Orion announces Orion EdgeGuard, a new industrial monitoring platform with notably similar features and a distributed inference architecture that look strikingly similar to LuminaSense's proprietary system. While proving direct IP theft in court would be expensive, slow, and uncertain, the damage to LuminaSense is immediate. The tight organizational integration between Nebula Ventures and Orion's Advanced Research Group made a strict informational firewall practically impossible. Even *if* no source code was copied, the visibility Orion gained into LuminaSense's architectural choices, failure modes, and prior dead ends allowed Orion's internal teams to accelerate their roadmap and sidestep years of trial-and-error. Inside Orion, Nebula Ventures is still praised and rewarded for having "scouted" a critical architecture and de-risked a new product line. This is despite the fact that their actions have severely undermined the competitive position of their own portfolio company. After all, the value to Orion of an entirely new business line is much more than the small check Nebula committed to LuminaSense.

Positive Scenario: The "Gold Standard" CVC and the Alignment of Interests

CareFlow Labs, an early-stage healthcare IT startup building a care-coordination and analytics platform that layers on top of existing Electronic Health Record (EHR) systems, receives investment from Northstar Capital, the corporate venture arm of Northstar Health Alliance, a multi-state hospital and outpatient clinic network. Northstar Capital exemplifies the "gold standard" CVC structure: it is set up as a separate legal entity with its own dedicated fund, independent investment committee, and a mandate that heavily weights financial returns alongside strategic fit with Northstar's long-term digital health strategy. Northstar Capital not only invests but also provides high-value introductions across the Northstar system, helping CareFlow launch pilots in several flagship hospitals and specialty clinics.

The structural separation allows for a sophisticated and disciplined approach to confidentiality. CareFlow signs one NDA with Northstar Capital that covers its financials, cap table, product roadmap, and other sensitive corporate information necessary for investment diligence. It signs a separate, tightly scoped mutual NDA directly with Northstar Health Alliance, limited to the technical specifications, workflow maps, and integration details needed to connect CareFlow's software into Northstar's EHR and scheduling infrastructure. Later, when a top-tier institutional VC expresses interest in leading CareFlow's Series A at a strong step-up valuation, Northstar Capital is fully supportive, because the higher valuation maximizes their financial return and validates their thesis. They do not pressure CareFlow into an early, below-market acquisition by Northstar; their incentive structure is aligned with driving the best overall outcome for all shareholders. In fact, Northstar Capital goes further, leveraging its network to introduce CareFlow to digital health teams and venture arms at competing hospital systems, helping the startup expand its commercial footprint well beyond Northstar's own walls.

Understanding the structure and motivations of a potential CVC investor is not a mere formality; it is a critical exercise in assessing the fundamental alignment of interests. It is about choosing a partner whose operational model, financial incentives, and legal framework will support, not hinder, your startup's journey to success. The "dumb money" label is an oversimplification; the truly intelligent founder digs deeper to find the "strategic, aligned money."

At this point, it is necessary to address a primary concern for startups engaging with CVCs: the risk that an NDA may be disregarded and a startup's ideas appropriated by the parent company to create a competing product. While failed startups have often leveled such accusations, in most Western CVC deals, these claims are difficult to substantiate. However, a series of high-profile lawsuits against one major American tech company suggests a pattern of behavior that, at the very least, tests the boundaries of ethical information use. Furthermore, this risk is not uniform across the globe. As will be discussed in a later chapter, Chinese CVCs have been extensively documented engaging in this practice. This book will not offer a legal opinion on the validity of these claims, but serves as a reminder to founders to exercise extreme caution in what they share, and to seek absolute clarity on how and with whom their information will be shared within the corporate structure, recognizing that the CVC's structure has very real implications for how that data will be used.

Note

1 Liz Arrington, "Most CVCs Invest from the Balance Sheet but Models Range from Ad Hoc to Near-Independent," *Global Corporate Venturing*, January 1, 2023, https://globalventuring.com/corporate/corporates-invest-from-the-balance-sheet/

Chapter 3

Beyond the Fund

Engaging Corporate Incubators, Accelerators, and Innovation Labs

A corporation's quest for innovation often extends beyond traditional venture capital investments. While corporate venture capital (CVC) funds act as financial and strategic partners to established startups, many corporations seek to engage with the innovation ecosystem at a much earlier, more formative stage. They dive deeper into the primordial soup of entrepreneurship by building dedicated innovation arms: incubators, accelerators, and internal innovation labs designed to work with entrepreneurs from the moment of inception. These innovation arms are an attempt to tap into the speed and agility of the startup world, often as a defensive measure against disruption and a way to inject entrepreneurial culture into a large, established organization.

Understanding these entities is critical for founders, as they represent a fundamentally different type of opportunity and a different set of risks compared to a CVC. A crucial distinction to grasp from the outset is their core motivation. Unlike most CVC funds that balance strategic and financial goals, corporate innovation arms are almost exclusively focused on **strategic value**.

Typically situated within a corporation's Research & Development (R&D) or Chief Strategy Officer's division rather than in finance or M&A, these groups are run as "cost centers." Their performance is not measured by the internal rate of return (IRR) of their investments, but by the volume and quality of innovation, market intelligence, and new capabilities they generate for the parent company. This structural reality shapes every interaction a startup will have with the corporation, as it provides different incentives and potentially vastly different strategic outcomes than traditional CVC investment.

Defining the Landscape: Incubators Versus Accelerators

The terms "incubator" and "accelerator" are often used interchangeably, but they describe distinct models of support tailored to different stages of a startup's life.

DOI: 10.4324/9781003758280-4

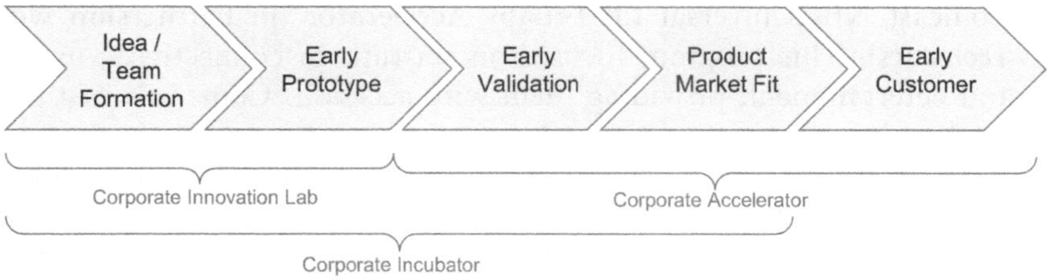

Exhibit 3.1 A timeline showing when different corporate innovation programs are best suited for a startup according to its maturity.

Corporate Incubators: An incubator, true to its name, is designed to "incubate" or protect and nurture a fledgling concept in its earliest days. It is a place for ideas that are often pre-product, pre-team, and pre-company. The goal is to provide a sheltered environment with resources, mentorship, and domain expertise to help an entrepreneur or a small team explore a problem space, validate a hypothesis, and incubate a raw idea until it hatches into a viable business concept. Engagements are often longer, less structured, and not necessarily cohort-based. They can often be highly focused on solving a specific corporate problem or need, and while this is great for determining early product-market fit, it is important for startups to keep their framework extensible so that it can work for other competing companies as well, rather than effectively becoming an outsourced consulting solution.

Corporate Accelerators: An accelerator, by contrast, aims to take an existing early-stage company and rapidly "accelerate" its growth over a fixed period. These programs are designed for startups that typically have a founding team, a minimum viable product (MVP), and perhaps some early signs of traction. Accelerators are intensive, cohort-based programs (usually lasting three to six months) that provide mentorship, educational programming, and networking opportunities, culminating in a "Demo Day" where the startups pitch to a broader audience of investors, including the CVC arm of the parent company and external VCs. These programs provide a fantastic opportunity to rapidly test a startup's assumptions about customer needs and willingness to pay, and in most cases, result in the startup graduating with its first customer. Like corporate incubators, however, it is important to avoid overspecializing your product for one specific customer and still keep it extensible and capable enough to sell to other customers.

Notable Corporate Accelerators and Incubators

Here are some prominent examples of corporate innovation programs that primarily work with external startups:

- **Comcast NBCUniversal LIFT Labs Accelerator (in Partnership with Techstars)**: This program focuses on startups in connectivity, media, and entertainment, providing them with access to Comcast's vast network of business units.
- **BMW Startup Garage**: This program operates on a "venture client" model, aiming to become a startup's first major customer and help mature their product through direct collaboration with BMW's engineering and business units.
- **Microsoft for Startups Founders Hub—Pegasus Program**: A platform offering free access to technology (including Azure credits), coaching, and support, designed to foster an ecosystem built on Microsoft's platforms.

Due Diligence for Innovation Programs

Before engaging with a corporate incubator or accelerator, it is crucial to conduct thorough due diligence on the terms of the program, as the terms can vary wildly. These programs are not a charity; they are a strategic transaction. You must ask critical questions of your legal counsel and the program managers. Key questions to ask include:

- **Intellectual Property (IP)**: Who owns the IP developed during the program? Does the corporation take any ownership or licensing rights?
- **Equity**: What percentage of equity, if any, does the corporation take in exchange for participation? (e.g., 7% for $120,000, as popularized by YCombinator)
- **Employment Status**: Are you classified as an employee of the corporation or your startup during the program?
- **Obligations**: What are your legal, social, and reporting obligations during and after the program? It is important to note that some programs, while not explicitly requiring it, expect their portfolio companies to regularly report or present to management.

These terms, often buried in the fine print, can have a far greater impact on your company's future than the small check you receive.

The Rise of Internal Innovation Labs and EIRs

In addition to externally facing accelerators and internally or externally facing incubators, many corporations have established internal "Innovation Groups" or "Labs." These serve a dual purpose: they are a defense mechanism against disruption and a magnet for talent.

First, they are an attempt to solve the "Innovator's Dilemma" and combat the "not invented here" (NIH) syndrome that plagues many large organizations. By creating a space for disruptive innovation inside the company, they allow corporations to explore new technologies and business models that might otherwise be stifled by the core business's operational inertia.

Second, they are a powerful tool for talent acquisition and retention. These labs enable talented and entrepreneurial employees to become **Entrepreneurs in Residence (EIRs)**, giving them the freedom to build something new without having to leave the security of the parent company. This prevents the brain drain of ambitious employees who might otherwise depart to found a competing startup. It also attracts top external talent who seek the thrill of a startup environment but value the resources and stability of a large institution.

Examples of Corporate Innovation Labs

- **Google's Area 120**: A well-known example of a lab created to allow Google employees to work on experimental new products and businesses full-time.
- **Microsoft Garage**: A comprehensive program that empowers Microsoft employees to work on passion projects, providing physical workshop spaces, access to tools and experts, and a structured program for experimentation and incubation.
- **Adobe Kickbox**: A highly regarded and innovative program where Adobe provides any interested employee with a literal red box containing a prepaid credit card for $1,000 and a step-by-step guide to developing and validating a new idea.
- **Nestlé's InGenius**: An employee-focused innovation accelerator where employees can submit ideas and secure funding and a six-month period to develop their project.
- **Google's 20% Time**: Although not explicitly a corporate innovation lab, Google famously used to grant employees an option to work on new projects one day a week. These often later graduated into new product lines at Google.

However, many programs like this last only for as long as their advocates are in a strategic position of power. Many similar programs, such as Walmart's Store No. 8, Barclays Rise, Capital One Labs, or Linked[In]cubator have either been shut down or absorbed or evolved into a broader corporate innovation strategy as budgets, leadership, and corporate priorities change. This ephemeral nature is a risk founders must consider.

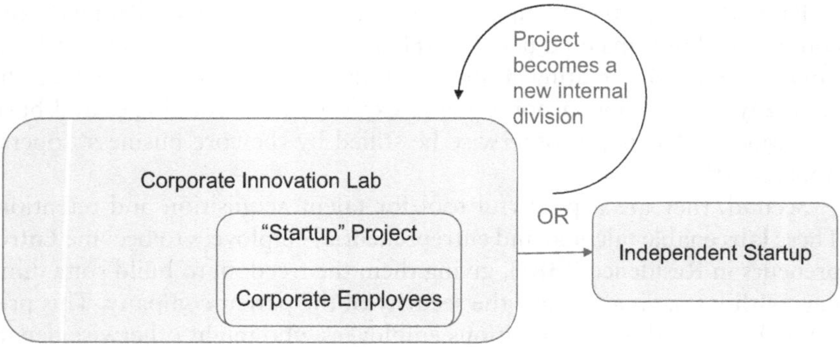

Exhibit 3.2 A diagram illustrating how startups inside a corporate innovation lab may either spin out or be recycled into a new division at the parent company.

For an individual with a powerful idea that serves a concentrated market but who hasn't yet built a company, these internal innovation labs can be an attractive option. They are particularly well-suited for undercapitalized founders who are more concerned with seeing their technology built than with having complete ownership and control. It can also be a good first step for new founders with a lower risk tolerance who are comfortable working within a large organization and cannot risk working without a salary for months or years.

This path, however, often looks less like founding a startup and more like an "intrapreneurship" track. Founders must go in with a clear understanding of what a successful "spin-out" process looks like, if one is allowed at all. Does the corporation help establish a new, independent legal entity? Do they become its first investor, taking a large equity stake (e.g., 30–50%) in exchange for the IP and resources they funded? Conversely, does the "successful" project simply become a new product line or a wholly owned subsidiary, with the founder reduced to a product manager? While this path provides financial security and a resource-rich environment, founders must be aware that their financial upside and ultimate control will be severely limited compared to a traditional venture-backed journey.

The Opportunity: An Unparalleled Path to Customer Discovery

For a startup at its earliest stages (pre-seed or seed round), engaging with one of these corporate innovation programs can be a game-changing opportunity. The value is not the small check or free office space they might provide, but the deep, immersive access to a potential cornerstone customer. They present a chance to move beyond theoretical customer personas and work directly with the business units, engineers, and end-users inside a major corporation.

Imagine a B2B SaaS startup struggling with customer discovery. By joining a corporate accelerator, they can get weekly access to the exact business unit they hope to sell to. They can shadow employees, map their workflows, and identify their most costly pain points, all before writing a single line of code for their main product. This direct feedback loop allows a startup to co-create its product with its ideal customer, dramatically de-risking product development and leading to a solution that has validated product-market fit from day one. Securing a pilot or a paid proof-of-concept (PoC) through one of these programs provides not only crucial early revenue but also a powerful signal of validation to future institutional investors. Founders must simply be cautious to ensure that these benefits don't have too many undue obligations attached to them.

The Founder's Dilemma: Navigating the Strategic Risks

The unparalleled access offered by these programs is, however, a double-edged sword. Because their primary mandate is strategic value for the parent, a fundamental tension exists that founders must navigate with extreme care.

The Overfitting Trap: Building a Feature, Not a Company

The greatest risk of embedding too deeply with a single corporate partner is "overfitting" your solution to their niche requirements. The relentless focus on solving one customer's specific problems can lead founders to build a highly customized product that is more of a consulting project than a scalable, venture-backable business. Founders might build the perfect feature for the parent corporation, but in doing so, may neglect the features and flexibility needed to sell to the broader market, or at the very least, build substantial "technology debt" into the product's core architecture that makes it much harder to pivot. This overfitting can inadvertently turn a startup into an outsourced R&D team, killing its potential to become a large, independent company.

The Confidentiality Conundrum: Information and Conflicts of Interest

The strategic nature of these programs means the informational firewall between the innovation arm and the parent company can be highly porous, if it exists at all. Startups will be encouraged to share openly with mentors and business units from the parent. While this facilitates co-creation, it also means the startup's proprietary information is being shared with an entity whose financial incentives are not aligned with theirs. This includes not just technical architecture, but pricing strategies, customer pipeline, hiring plans, and the startup's strategic vulnerabilities.

The incubator, accelerator, or innovation group's ultimate loyalty is to their corporate parent, which creates a clear conflict of interest. Will the program managers help a startup partner with the parent company's chief competitor? Will they advocate for the startup to take a higher valuation from an outside investor if it complicates the parent's future acquisition options? The answer is likely no, because their success is measured by the parents' success, not the success of the startup. In general, it is best for founders to keep the conversation focused on what the customer wants them to do and if they can do it. Avoid discussions of *how* the startup does what it does. This gives the corporate the information they need to work with the startup, but not the information needed to replicate the startup's work.

Before engaging with a corporate innovation program, founders must go in with their eyes wide open. These programs can provide an incredible launchpad, but they are not a substitute for a diverse customer base and an independent vision. The smart founder uses them as a tool: leverage their access for deep learning and initial validation, secure that first marquee customer logo, but always maintain a clear-eyed focus on building a scalable company for a broad market, protecting their intellectual property, and retaining the strategic freedom to control their own destiny.

Chapter 4

When Is the Right Time to Engage a CVC?

In venture capital, as in so many aspects of business, timing is critical. For a startup founder, the timing of their fundraising approach can dramatically influence its outcome. Initiating a conversation with an institutional VC too early, before key milestones are met, can lead to a premature "no." An early negative data point can be difficult to overcome when reapproaching the same firm later. Starting too late, on the other hand, can mean fundraising from a position of weakness, with dwindling cash reserves eroding a founder's leverage in negotiations and leading to less favorable terms.

When engaging with a corporate venture capital (CVC) arm, this calculus of timing becomes even more complex and strategically vital. The decision is no longer solely about financial readiness; it is about strategic maturity and the potential for synergy. A CVC is not just another source of capital; it is a potential strategic partner, and the nature of that partnership dictates the optimal moment for engagement. Approaching a CVC at the right time, when your product is ready for enterprise scale, and your team is prepared for the demands of a corporate partnership, can unlock immense value far beyond the capital invested. Conversely, approaching at the wrong time can lead to a frustrating, time-consuming exercise that distracts from the core mission of building the company, with little to show for the effort. This chapter provides a framework for navigating this critical decision.

Universal Principles for Engagement

Before we segment our advice by startup type, there are several universal principles that apply to any founder contemplating a conversation with a CVC. These principles are foundational to a successful engagement and, if ignored, can lead to significant wasted effort and strategic missteps.

DOI: 10.4324/9781003758280-5

Define Your "Why" Before the First Meeting: The Partnership Thesis

You must enter the conversation with a clear-eyed and well-articulated understanding of what you hope to gain from the relationship, beyond the capital. It is not enough to have a vague notion of "strategic value." You must develop a concrete "Partnership Thesis." This thesis should be a clear, concise articulation of the potential value exchange between your startup and the CVC's parent corporation.

- **Identify Your Primary Goal**: Is your most critical objective to land the parent corporation as a marquee customer to validate your product and unlock future sales? Are you seeking access to their unique distribution channels to enter a new geography or customer segment that would otherwise be inaccessible? Do you need their specialized laboratories, manufacturing expertise, or proprietary datasets to validate and scale your technology? Or is your main objective the powerful reputational halo that comes from their globally recognized brand, validating your startup in a crowded market?
- **Remain Open to Discovery**: While it is essential to have this initial hypothesis, you must also remain open to discovering new avenues of collaboration. As you learn more about the CVC and its parent during the meeting, you may uncover less-obvious capabilities or pressing strategic needs that present an even greater opportunity. The best partnerships are born from a combination of your prepared agenda and a willingness to explore unforeseen synergies. Your initial thesis is the starting point for the conversation, not a rigid, unchangeable plan.

The Three-Month Rule: Cultivate Your Champion Early

As a general rule of thumb, it is wise to begin conversations with CVCs at least three months before you plan to formally kick off your fundraising round. This extended timeline is necessary primarily because CVCs, as a rule, move more slowly than their institutional counterparts. Their decision-making process is often more complex, involving a web of stakeholders beyond the investment team.

- **Navigating the Corporate Labyrinth**: A potential investment may need to be reviewed and blessed by the heads of relevant business units, the corporate strategy team, senior legal counsel, and sometimes even the CEO or CFO of the parent company. Each of these stakeholders has their own priorities and concerns, and building consensus takes time. According to a 2024 report by Silicon Valley Bank,[1] only 19% of CVCs are able to make investment decisions without approval from the parent company, regardless of their structure. This approval will take time.

- **The Role of the Internal Champion**: Your primary contact at the CVC must act as an "internal champion," shepherding your deal through this complex process. Starting early gives this champion the time they need to have informal conversations, socialize your company with key decision-makers, and build the internal coalition of support necessary to get a deal approved. Rushing this process can force your champion to present your case before the groundwork has been laid, significantly increasing the chances of a "no."
- **Time for Strategic Negotiation**: This extended timeline also provides the necessary runway to negotiate the strategic terms that will likely end up in a side letter. The side letter process can be as involved and time-consuming as negotiating the financial terms themselves.

Manage Your Expectations: The Co-Investor Mindset

While there are exceptions, most CVCs prefer to act as co-investors, following a reputable institutional VC that takes the lead on setting the financial terms. As lead investors customarily take a board seat, it is generally preferable to have an institutional VC lead the round, with the CVC acting as an endorsement of your company, rather than the primary investor. It is a strategic error to build your fundraising strategy around the assumption that a CVC will be your lead investor.

- **Leveraging the Lead's Diligence**: CVCs often lack the large, dedicated teams for financial modeling and legal term sheet negotiation that institutional VCs possess. They prefer to leverage the rigorous financial due diligence and term-setting performed by a lead institutional investor, allowing them to focus their own resources on assessing the strategic fit and potential for partnership.
- **The "Keeping Them Warm" Strategy**: Because CVCs take time to build consensus internally and are simultaneously not likely to lead, the most effective approach is to engage CVCs early, build a relationship, and explore the strategic fit in detail. Keep them periodically updated on your progress (e.g., with a brief monthly or quarterly email highlighting key achievements that you are already sending to other investors you are keeping warm). Once you have a term sheet from a lead institutional investor, you can then re-engage the CVC with a clear valuation and timeline. This allows them to move much more quickly, as the financial terms are already set and they have already done the preliminary work of understanding your company and building internal support. Approval processes may still make them one of the last checks to close in your round, however.

Founders should also expect that early conversations with a corporate venture team may include several participants from different divisions: business development, technical, and investment functions. Ideally the CVC will inform you of the participants in advance so you can better prepare, but don't be surprised if there are some extra ears in the call. This isn't a sign of disorganization or overkill; it usually means the sponsor wants to align all stakeholders early and accelerate approvals. Don't be intimidated by a crowded call. Diverse attendance is often a signal of genuine internal interest, not bureaucracy. However, do be cautious about the information you choose to share with employees of the parent company, rather than their venture capital arm.

The Right Time for Market-Ready Startups

For startups with a product that is ready to sell and a primary goal of scaling revenue, the timing of CVC engagement hinges on your readiness to partner with a large, complex enterprise. This is a critical distinction: having a product that works is not the same as having a product that is ready for a corporate environment.

Are You Truly "Enterprise-Ready"?

Having a product that is "ready to sell" means more than just having functional code. For a large corporate partner, "ready" implies a level of robustness, security, and support that early-stage products often lack. Before approaching a CVC with the goal of a commercial partnership, you must honestly assess your enterprise-readiness across several domains:

- **Technical Integration and Scalability**: Can your product seamlessly plug into their complex, often legacy, tech stack?
    - **APIs and Documentation**: Have you built robust, well-documented Application Programming Interfaces (APIs) that their engineering teams can easily work with? Is your documentation clear, comprehensive, and professional?
    - **Scalability and Reliability**: Can your infrastructure handle the load of a large corporate user base? Have you stress-tested your systems? A pilot that crashes can be a fatal blow to a future commercial relationship.
- **Security and Compliance**: Large corporations operate under intense regulatory scrutiny and have stringent security requirements. A failure here is a non-starter.
    - **Security Audits**: Have you undergone third-party security audits, such as a SOC 2 or ISO 27001 certification? Being able to produce these reports is often a prerequisite for even starting a technical discussion.

- **Data Handling and Privacy**: Are you prepared to answer detailed, granular questions about your data handling, encryption, and privacy policies? Do you comply with regulations like General Data Protection Regulation (GDPR) or California Consumer Privacy Act (CCPA)? A vague answer here may immediately disqualify you.

- **Support and Implementation Capacity**: A corporate partner is not a self-service customer. They will demand a high level of support.
  - **Dedicated Resources**: Do you have the internal capacity to support a large-scale pilot or deployment? This often means having dedicated support engineers, a project manager, and a solutions architect who can manage the implementation process.
  - **Service-Level Agreements (SLAs)**: Are you prepared to commit to and meet enterprise-grade SLAs for uptime and support response times?

While requirements will vary from corporate to corporate and project to project, be ready for these kinds of questions and have answers. If the answer is no, make sure that you have at least a rough outline of when you plan to reach that level of readiness. Make sure you understand what the needs of a corporate are before diving deep into negotiating project scopes.

Are You Ready for the Corporate Sales Cycle?

Engaging with a large corporation as a customer is a marathon, not a sprint. The sales cycle is notoriously long and labyrinthine, often involving a "buying committee" of stakeholders from different departments, each with their own agenda and concerns.

- **Navigating the Bureaucracy**: It is not uncommon for a corporate to have more people working on their side of a potential deal, from procurement, legal, and IT security to the end business unit, than you have employees in your entire company. Each of these departments can raise objections or create delays. Procurement will negotiate on price, legal will scrutinize every clause of the contract, and IT will demand extensive security reviews. The number of meetings and questions from various departments can be overwhelming for the busy schedules of startup founders.
- **The Need for a Dedicated Point Person**: This is why it is often best to engage when you have hired a dedicated business development or sales professional who can act as the single point of contact for corporate partners. This individual's full-time job is to manage these complex relationships, navigate the internal bureaucracy, and shield the CEO and product team from the immense time suck of a corporate procurement

process. If you are a founder still handling all sales yourself, you may be too early to effectively leverage a corporate partnership. The time and energy required to close a single corporate deal can easily distract a founder from the more critical tasks of product development and company building, putting the entire startup at risk.

The Right Time for Deep Tech and Niche Innovators

For startups in deep tech sectors like biotechnology, advanced materials, or semiconductors, the engagement calculus is different. The same is true for companies serving highly concentrated customer bases with extensive customization needs, such as in the defense or aerospace industries. For these ventures, the focus is less on immediate, scalable sales and more on deep technology validation, co-development, and securing a foundational customer relationship.

Is Your IP Defensible and Your Technology Validated?

For these startups, a CVC is not investing in a finished product; they are investing in an implementable technological vision. They may take informational meetings with "science project" companies that are still working on big ideas on paper, but most are only investing in a potential breakthrough that has been sufficiently de-risked to be considered a viable commercial endeavor. This means you should engage only after key technical and legal milestones have been met.

- **Intellectual Property Strategy**: Your core intellectual property must be developed and, ideally, protected. This doesn't just mean filing a provisional patent. It means having a clear IP strategy. Is your competitive advantage based on a portfolio of patents, or is it a closely guarded trade secret? You must be able to articulate this strategy and demonstrate that you have taken the necessary steps to defend your technological moat. A technology-focused CVC will conduct extensive IP diligence, and any ambiguity here can kill a deal.
- **Tangible Proof-of-Concept**: You must have early, tangible technical results that demonstrate your approach works. This is the evidence that separates a promising idea from a venture-investable technology. This proof can take many forms: compelling data from lab experiments that have been replicated (especially by independent labs), a working benchtop prototype that demonstrates the core function, or a successful simulation that has been validated against real-world data. You must be able to prove that the fundamental science is sound and that the primary challenge has shifted from "can it work?" to "how do we scale it and integrate it into their systems?"

Are You Seeking a Joint Development Partner?

Often, the most valuable contribution a CVC can make to a deep tech startup is not an immediate sales channel but a **Joint Development Agreement (JDA)**. The purpose of a JDA is largely to test how your technology can scale and integrate into the systems of the parent company. In this process, the parent corporation can provide invaluable resources that are impossible for a startup to access on its own. This could include specialized manufacturing lines for pilot production runs, unique and proprietary datasets for training AI models, access to world-class scientists with decades of domain experience, or guidance in navigating complex regulatory pathways like those of the Food and Drug Administration (FDA) or Federal Aviation Administration (FAA).

The CVC investment often serves as the crucial first step before a paid JDA, where the parent company funds further development in exchange for early access or specific rights to the technology. The right time to engage is when you have a clear vision for what this JDA would entail. You should be able to articulate precisely how the corporate's resources would accelerate your technical and commercial roadmap, or how a JDA would improve your technology readiness and bring it closer to integration readiness with the corporate.

The CVC's investment, in this context, becomes a powerful dual signal to the market. It shows that an industry leader has not only financially backed your company but is also becoming a deep technical and commercial partner. For these startups, the CVC is the ultimate customer discovery tool, providing unparalleled insight into the real-world needs and challenges your technology aims to solve.

It is critical, however, to maintain a clean separation between the equity investment and the JDA. As we will discuss in the chapter on side letters, do not accept a deal that uses the investment as a way for the corporate to get a "free" or discounted JDA. The two agreements should be able to stand on their own financial and strategic merits.

Lastly, it is sometimes easier to secure an investment *after* a JDA is already signed. This dramatically de-risks the proposition for the CVC, as the strategic buy-in from the parent company is already confirmed. In this scenario, the primary advantage of the CVC's investment shifts from being a catalyst for the partnership to being a powerful public signal of that partnership's success. At the same time, if a JDA is already signed, it somewhat reduces the strategic imperative for investment, as the strategic value has already been secured. In effect, there is much less marginal strategic value generated by making an investment after the JDA is already signed. Asking the VC whether the investment or the JDA is usually negotiated and signed first can give a valuable insight into which is worth prioritizing first.

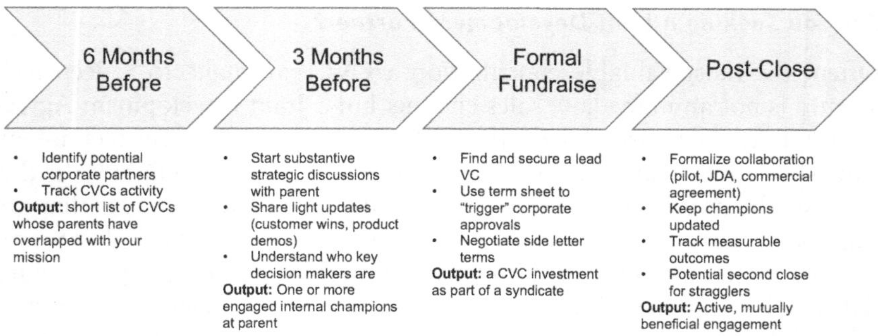

Exhibit 4.1 A diagram showing the timeline of engagements between startups and CVCs.

Accommodating Slower Timelines: Bridges and Extensions

While the ideal fundraising scenario involves all investors participating simultaneously in a single, clean, priced-round, the reality of a CVC's slower operational cadence can make this challenging. If a CVC is highly interested but cannot complete its internal approval process in time to join the main financing round, a founder has several tools at their disposal to accommodate them without derailing the entire process.

These mechanisms, often structured as a **bridge round** or a **round extension**, typically involve the CVC investing at a later date through a convertible instrument like a Simple Agreement for Future Equity (SAFE) or a convertible note. This approach can also be highly effective for engaging CVCs between priced rounds, either when a significant strategic collaboration opportunity arises or when a CVC initiates contact with a compelling partnership thesis.

However, these instruments introduce their own set of complexities that founders must navigate carefully. The primary goal is to secure the strategic partner without creating undue friction with existing investors or distracting the leadership team from the core business. Offering a CVC the same valuation and terms as the previous round may be perceived as "unfair" by existing investors, who took on significantly more risk by investing earlier. Conversely, setting a higher price could be interpreted by the market as a formal "re-pricing" of the company, setting a new valuation expectation for the next full round.

Bridge rounds are often viewed with skepticism by institutional VCs; traditionally seen as a consequence of a cash crunch or missed milestones. However, it is increasingly common for startups to engage in small "strategic bridge rounds" comprising one or two CVCs. The narrative of these rounds then shifts from a negative connotation of distress to a positive one of business development and commercial traction. It signals that an eager customer is investing to solidify a strategic alliance, a powerful validation that can actually build momentum for the next priced round.

Ultimately, any such financing will require the approval of the company's Board of Directors. The board, along with experienced legal counsel, can provide invaluable guidance in structuring the bridge or extension in a way that balances the strategic benefit of bringing on the CVC with the need to be fair to existing shareholders and maintain a clean and logical financing history for the company.

Corporate venture partnerships reward preparation. The founders who succeed are those who treat timing not as a matter of luck but by design. The best founders engage CVCs when their company, product, and internal processes are ready to absorb the complexities of a corporate partnership. With the right structure, even a delayed or extended close can strengthen the relationship, rather than strain it. Now that you have a CVC's attention and time, the next challenge lies in how to negotiate, align incentives, and formalize the partnership that follows.

Note

1 Silicon Valley Bank and Counterpart Ventures, *State of CVC 2024: 2024 CVC Survey Key Findings*, September 2024, https://www.svb.com/globalassets/trendsandinsights/reports/the-state-of-corporate-venture-capital-2024-report.pdf

Chapter 5

Decoding the Side Letter

Common Partnership Terms

The terms of a venture capital investment are typically memorialized in a suite of standardized documents, often based on templates from respected organizations like the National Venture Capital Association (NVCA). These definitive agreements, including a Stock Purchase Agreement, an Investors' Rights Agreement (IRA), and a Voting Agreement, form the legal bedrock of the relationship between a startup and its investors. For a comprehensive breakdown of these standard documents, the NVCA website, as well as the numerous books available on fundraising, remains an indispensable resource. This book, however, will focus on the terms that are unique to corporate venture capital (CVC) firms: The bespoke provisions more commonly found not in the term sheet itself, but in a parallel, and equally important, document: the side letter.

First, What Are Side Letters?

In the course of financing, situations frequently arise where a specific investor requires rights, privileges, or obligations that fall outside the scope of the main agreements or are not intended to apply to all investors in the round. This is where a side letter comes into play. A side letter is a supplementary contract, executed between the company and one or more specific investors, that grants tailored contractual rights "on the side" of the primary financing documentation.

While institutional VCs might use a side letter to grant, for example, major investor rights to a smaller fund that doesn't meet the official threshold, CVCs have transformed the side letter into a primary instrument of strategic alignment. Driven by their dual strategic and financial imperatives, CVCs utilize side letters as a crucial mechanism to secure terms directly linked to their parent corporation's goals. These are terms that might be irrelevant, or even objectionable, to the purely financial co-investors participating in the same financing round. The side letter provides a flexible and often confidential vehicle for the CVC to secure these bespoke rights.

DOI: 10.4324/9781003758280-6

Rights that a CVC may want may include enhanced information access for market intelligence, rights of first refusal on a potential acquisition, or specific terms governing a commercial partnership.

While they remain "on the side," it is critical to understand that side letters are fully enforceable, legally binding contracts. However, their enforcement mechanisms and relationship to the main agreements require careful consideration. A breach of a side letter provision might not automatically constitute an event of default under the main financing documents. This means the available remedies might be limited to standard breach of contract actions (e.g., seeking damages or specific performance) rather than triggering the broader protective mechanisms, such as the acceleration of debt, built into the core agreements. Side letters should explicitly state whether they prevail in the event of a conflict with the main financing document.

A foundational principle for founders and their legal counsel should be the pursuit of simplicity and clarity in all legal documents. A "clean" term sheet, free of overly complex or non-standard terms, is always preferable. For this reason, NVCA has created a set of example "NVCA standard" documents for a clean financing round. This principle extends with equal, if not greater, force to side letters. Each additional clause adds a layer of complexity and potential for future conflict or misinterpretation. The goal should be to use the side letter as a tool to define the strategic relationship, not as a repository for convoluted or extraneous rights that could encumber the company down the line.

A final, critical note of caution: even *if* a side letter is drafted as a confidential agreement, its existence and core terms are rarely a secret for long. When one investor receives special rights, other major investors in the round will often invoke their own "Most Favored Nation" (MFN) rights for the financing round, demanding the same privileges and creating a level playing field. For example, if a CVC with a $5 million check in a round demands major investor rights, the institutional investor who put in $7 million, but is still below the "major investor" threshold, will likely want those major investor rights too. Therefore, founders must negotiate every side letter term with the assumption that it could eventually be granted to all institutional investors. This dynamic forces a founder to consider not just the impact of granting a right to one CVC, but the cumulative, and potentially burdensome, effect of granting it to the entire syndicate. For this reason, it is a sound strategy to keep side letter terms strictly limited to strategic collaboration objectives, rather than granting any specific or unusual financial rights. Note: MFN clauses in financing documents are standard. They ensure that all investors in a round are getting the same deal. MFNs for commercial contracts are a different beast, to be discussed later.

Common Strategic Terms in CVC Side Letters

The following are common terms CVCs request in side letters, ranging from the relatively benign to the potentially hazardous for a startup's long-term health.

Deal Term: Assignment Rights

Mechanics: This clause defines the CVC's ability to "assign" or transfer its investment rights to another party: both its shares and, more importantly, its special contractual rights from the side letter (e.g., information rights, observer rights, vetoes). The scope can range from a very narrow right to assign only to wholly owned subsidiaries of the parent, to a broad right to assign to any "affiliate" or "successor," which could include future, unknown acquirers of the CVC or its parent's divisions.

CVC Motivation: Large corporations are not static; they are constantly reorganizing, spinning off divisions, creating new subsidiaries, or acquiring other companies. The CVC seeks assignment rights to maintain flexibility. They want the ability to move the startup investment to the most logical home within their complex and evolving corporate structure without needing to seek the startup's consent for every internal transfer. It is a clause sought for operational and administrative convenience.

Implications for a Startup: This term is a generally innocuous boilerplate term. The primary danger is that a trusted, friendly CVC partner could, through a corporate transaction completely outside of your control, be replaced by a hostile or conflicted new partner. An unrestricted assignment right could allow the CVC to transfer its powerful side letter rights to a division of the parent that becomes a direct competitor, or worse, to an external company that acquires that division. A founder could wake up one day to find their biggest rival now has a contractual right to their most sensitive company information. More likely, however, is the risk of "strategic alignment decay," where the valuable connections to relevant parts of a CVC's parent organization are severed, or at the very least, no longer incentivized, as part of a restructuring.

Recommendations for Startups: Avoid a broad, unrestricted assignment right. Any assignment provision is ideally aggressively narrowed with the following limitations:

- **Limit to Wholly Owned Subsidiaries**: The CVC should only be able to assign its rights to entities that are 100% owned and controlled by the ultimate parent company.
- **Include a Competitor Blacklist**: The clause must explicitly state that no rights can be assigned to any entity that is a competitor of the startup.

- **Add a Termination Provision**: Crucially, the clause should state that if an assignee *later* becomes a competitor (e.g., through a subsequent merger), all special rights (information, observer, etc.) automatically terminate. These termination provisions may be difficult to attain, but can be a robust form of protection.

Deal Term: Board Observer Rights

Mechanics: Board observer rights grant the CVC the ability to designate an individual (the "observer") who is entitled to attend all meetings of the startup's Board of Directors. In addition to attending meetings, the observer typically receives the same information package (board deck, financials, minutes) distributed to the voting directors. Crucially, an observer cannot vote on any board matters, is not counted for the purpose of establishing a quorum, and, most importantly, **does not owe a fiduciary duty** to the company or its shareholders. Their legal and fiduciary obligation remains with their employer, the CVC, and its parent corporation. Note: some institutional VCs will ask for a board observer seat in addition to their board director seat. This is commonly used to train junior members of the team who eventually become the primary channel for communication between the startup and the fund. The use of board observers for CVCs is notably different.

CVC Motivation: The primary motivation for seeking observer rights is to gain a deeper, real-time insight into the company's strategy, operations, and governance beyond what is available in standard quarterly reports. A seat at the table, even a non-voting one, provides unfiltered access to the board's deliberations, debates, and decision-making processes. This allows the CVC to monitor its investment more closely, get an early warning on potential challenges, and identify opportunities for strategic collaboration. Furthermore, even as a non-voting member, the observer can act as an advocate for the parent company's interests, influencing discussions on product roadmaps, market entry strategies, or potential partnerships in a way that aligns with the corporate parent's goals.

Implications for a Startup: This can be a double-edged sword. A constructive, well-aligned observer can be a valuable channel for strategic alignment, acting as a high-bandwidth conduit to the parent corporation's resources and expertise. However, because the observer's primary loyalty is to the CVC parent and they have no legal duty to act in your company's best interest, this arrangement carries some risk. The presence of an observer can "chill" open and candid discussion among the actual board members, who may be hesitant to discuss sensitive topics, such as a potential partnership with a competitor of the CVC's parent, with an outsider in the room.

It is best to grant these rights only to CVCs with strong information firewalls and a financial motivation that aligns their interests with yours. For example, a legally separate CVC arm with a GP/LP structure has an obligation to maximize its returns, rather than maximize strategic outcomes for their parent company. For others, it is far safer to offer alternatives like **Management Access** (regular, structured meetings with the executive team) or to form a **customer advisory board** where the CVC can provide feedback on product roadmaps without having access to confidential board-level strategy. If an observer seat is unavoidable, consider adding a provision in the side letter that allows the board to excuse the observer from any portion of a meeting where a potential conflict of interest is being discussed.

Positive Scenario: The Strategic Conduit

The Setup: MedTech Innovate, a startup developing a new AI-powered diagnostic tool, accepts a Series A investment from HealthSystem Ventures, the financially motivated, separately incorporated CVC of a large hospital network. The CVC negotiates for a board observer seat, which is granted because of the clear strategic alignment and the CVC's strong reputation. The observer is a seasoned healthcare operator who works on the CVC's "platform" team, dedicated to helping portfolio companies.

The Interaction: During a board meeting, the MedTech CEO presents a plan to begin the long and arduous process of seeking regulatory approval in Europe. The CVC observer listens intently. After the formal presentation, she speaks up,

> Our parent organization just spent 18 months navigating the new EU medical device regulations for a different diagnostics device. I can connect you directly with the head of our regulatory affairs team in Berlin. They've already built the playbook and have relationships with the key notified bodies. This could save you at least a year and hundreds of thousands in consulting fees.

The Outcome: The observer makes the introduction. The MedTech team gets direct, actionable advice from world-class experts, dramatically accelerating their European go-to-market strategy. The observer acts as a true strategic conduit, translating the startup's needs into the corporate parent's resources. The partnership flourishes because the CVC's financial incentive (a successful European launch increases the startup's value) is perfectly aligned with the startup's goals.

Negative Scenario: The Conflicted Mole

The Setup: Nautilus Systems, a startup developing robotic automation tools for commercial fishing operations, raises its Series A round. As part of the investment, BlueHarbor Ventures, the CVC arm of Ocean-Fleet Industries, one of the world's largest manufacturers of commercial fishing vessels, negotiates a board observer seat. BlueHarbor sits within OceanFleet's corporate strategy group and operates with a strong strategic mandate: surface emerging technologies that could enhance or defend the parent's equipment business. Excited by industry validation, the founders accept the observer seat without defining exclusions for discussions involving future product lines that might overlap with OceanFleet's offerings.

The Interaction: A year later, Nautilus expands its product line from retrofits of existing fishing boats and begins development of a fully autonomous, small-form fishing craft designed for near-shore operations. At a board meeting, the CEO presents detailed launch plans: target regions, pricing, technical specs, and a pipeline of fisheries expressing interest in pre-orders. This new craft directly overlaps with OceanFleet's smaller fishing boat designs.

The BlueHarbor observer listens, asks a few product questions, and takes structured notes. As a board *observer*, not a fiduciary, he has no duty to withhold strategic intelligence from OceanFleet.

The Fallout: The observer briefs OceanFleet's commercial team, who interpret Nautilus' upcoming launch as competitive pressure. OceanFleet responds by offering several midsized fisheries a steep, time-limited bulk discount on its existing small-vessel line.

The move is routine defensive pricing, not sabotage, but it affects Nautilus' market. Fisheries that had been considering autonomous craft instead redirected their capital to secure OceanFleet's discounted boats in bulk. By launch time, the market segment Nautilus targeted is temporarily saturated. Sales cycles lengthen, unit economics tighten, and Nautilus loses the early-mover momentum it had built.

Institutional directors begin to notice that sensitive competitive discussions cannot be held freely with a CVC observer present. Board materials become segmented; pre-meetings increase; transparency declines.

Founder's Takeaway: A board observer is not a board member. They are an information channel for their firm, and you must operate under the assumption that everything they hear will be reported back. Before granting an observer seat, perform deep diligence on the CVC's structure and motivations. If their incentives are not financially aligned with yours, or if they lack a strong firewall with the parent, it is best to avoid this clause, or at the very least, require them to step out during discussion of sensitive and potentially conflicted topics (such as partnerships or sales to competitors).

Deal Term: Carve-outs from Non-Compete Agreements

Mechanics: In a typical acquisition, the acquirer requires the target company's key executives and major shareholders (including investors) to sign a non-compete agreement. This is a standard measure to prevent them from taking the proceeds from the sale and immediately starting or funding a new, competitive venture. A CVC will almost always use a side letter to negotiate a "carve-out" from this obligation, stipulating that while the CVC entity itself might be bound, its parent corporation and all of its affiliates are explicitly exempt from any non-compete restrictions.

CVC Motivation: The CVC's motivation here is absolute and non-negotiable: protecting the parent corporation's freedom to operate. A multi-billion-dollar conglomerate cannot have its global business strategy constrained because its venture arm sold a minority stake in a startup. The parent company must remain free to develop, manufacture, partner, or acquire any technology in any market, even if it is directly competitive with the company being acquired. This carve-out prevents a future acquirer from suing the CVC's parent for violating a non-compete that the CVC was forced to sign as part of a drag-along sale.

Implications for a Startup: While this term is standard and almost impossible for a founder to negotiate away, it may have some implications for potential acquirers, especially if that acquirer is a direct competitor to the CVC's parent company or if the acquirer's primary goal is often to gain an exclusive competitive advantage or moat. This carve-out means that even after buying the company, they cannot stop their chief rival (the CVC's parent) from continuing to compete in that exact space, potentially using knowledge gained during its time as an investor. This could potentially shrink the pool of potential acquirers by excluding those who were hoping to use an acquisition to gain a monopoly or corner a market, especially if the CVC's parent has a history of "fast following" innovative business models, and would be likely to replicate internally what you have built together if a partnership were to be terminated.

Negative Scenario: The AutoDrive AI Dilemma

The Setup: AutoDrive AI, a startup developing a cutting-edge Level 4 autonomous driving software stack using a novel and secret method, raises its Series B. The round is co-led by a top institutional VC and Global Motors Ventures (GMV), the CVC arm of a massive automaker. As a standard part of their investment, GMV's side letter includes a clear carve-out exempting Global Motors and all its subsidiaries from any future non-compete agreements related to the sale of AutoDrive AI.

The Acquisition Offer: Two years later, AutoDrive AI's technology is best-in-class, and they decide to explore an acquisition. Their dream acquirer is Trans-National Auto (TNA), a direct and fierce competitor to Global Motors. TNA sees acquiring AutoDrive AI as a once-in-a-decade opportunity to leapfrog Global Motors in the race to full autonomy, and they are prepared to pay a significant premium to "own" the technology and the market.

The Conflict: During the M&A due diligence process, TNA's legal team reviews the CVC side letter and discovers the non-compete carve-out. The strategic rationale for their premium offer immediately comes under fire. The TNA executive team realizes that even if they pay a premium to acquire AutoDrive AI, they cannot prevent Global Motors from continuing to develop its own autonomous systems using a similar architectural philosophy as AutoDrive AI. They worry that GMV's board observer seat and management access rights gave Global Motors an inside look at AutoDrive AI's roadmap, which they could, in time and with sufficient resources, replicate. The acquisition, although still likely to go through, may be at a more reasonable valuation depending on how much TNA believes GMV will now know about their roadmap from their information rights as an investor, and how quickly Global Motors would be able to build a competitor to AutoDrive AI in-house, given what they know.

The Fallout

1. **Valuation Hit:** TNA's M&A committee determines that they can no longer justify a premium "strategic coup d'etat" valuation. They lower their acquisition offer by 10%, reframing the deal as a "top technology and talent" acquisition rather than a "market-dominating" one that grants them an effective monopoly on self-driving.
2. **Reduced Leverage:** The AutoDrive AI board now has slightly less leverage. Their other potential acquirers are either smaller players who can't afford a premium price or non-automotive tech companies for whom the strategic value is lower.
3. **A Smaller Exit:** AutoDrive AI is now faced with a difficult choice: accept TNA's lower offer or walk away and hope another buyer emerges.

Founder's Takeaway: Unlike many of the more dangerous terms we will discuss in this and the following chapter, a non-compete carve-out for the CVC's parent is almost always a "must-have" for the CVC and is not a battle you are likely to win. The key is not to fight the term itself, but to understand its strategic consequences from the moment you take the CVC's money. An important question to ask is, "How much will the information I share with my CVC investor damage my potential acquisition price for their competitor?" Usually, it is not going to be much (if any at all) if you take proper precautions around information sharing, and thus will not have a big effect on acquisition. Be aware that the most logical and highest-paying acquirer for your company may *not* be a direct competitor of your CVC's parent. This understanding should inform your long-term strategy, your board composition, and the relationships you build across the industry, ensuring you are not blindsided when it is time to sell the company.

Deal Term: Change-of-Control Provisions—Change of Control of Startup

Mechanics: This clause defines the CVC's rights in the event that the startup itself is acquired, with a particular focus on acquisitions by a competitor of the CVC's parent company. Most commonly, change-of-control provisions give the corporate the right to terminate partnerships with the startup in the case of its acquisition by a competitor, especially projects related to information sharing. However, a corporate investor may request provisions that give it the right to veto or block a sale to a named competitor, allow it to require a buyout of its shares upon such a transaction, or grant special approval rights over any acquisition involving a competitor. These blocking rights are rare because of how powerful they are and how misaligned they are with the interests of the startup.

CVC Motivation: The CVC's primary motivation is defensive. The parent corporation has invested in the startup to gain a strategic advantage, be it access to technology, market intelligence, or a potential future acquisition target. Allowing a direct competitor to acquire the startup would not only negate this advantage but could actively turn it against them, as the competitor would gain control of the very asset the parent had nurtured, sometimes with their own data and company secrets. From the CVC's perspective, these provisions are a mechanism to safeguard their strategic interests.

Implications for a Startup: For a founder, these terms can have long-term implications for the future of the company. An acquisition could lead to a loss of, or a major rescoping of, a large key customer. An outright veto right can materially limit exit flexibility by shrinking the pool of potential acquirers and discouraging competitive bidding wars. The existence of an acquisition veto right, once discovered during an acquirer's due diligence, can "chill" M&A interest, as potential buyers will be reluctant to invest months of effort into a deal that a single shareholder can unilaterally block. This directly impedes the board's fiduciary duty to secure the best possible outcome for all shareholders.

Recommendations for Startups

- **Resist Veto Rights**: Outright veto rights are very founder-unfriendly and can hold your company hostage.
- **Offer Alternatives**: If a compromise is necessary, offer weaker rights such as a right to be consulted or receive advance notice of a sale, rather than a right to consent.

- **Narrowly Define "Competitor"**: If a clause references competitors, ensure the definition is extremely narrow and specific, ideally limited to a short, named list of companies. Avoid broad language like "any company engaged in the business of..."
- **Propose a Buyout Option**: A reasonable compromise can be to terminate all partnerships and delete data that could expose internal processes of the parent company, and/or to grant the CVC the right to have its shares bought out by the company or the acquirer in the event of a sale to a competitor, allowing them a clean exit without giving them the power to block the deal.

Negative Scenario: The Chilled Acquisition

The Setup: SecureLayer, a fast-growing startup providing advanced data protection infrastructure for enterprise cloud environments, raises its Series C round led by TeleComet Ventures, the investment arm of a major global telecommunications company. The side letter includes a clause giving TeleComet the right to veto any acquisition by three listed competitors in the cloud infrastructure space.

The Interaction: Two years later, SecureLayer's encryption engine becomes the market leader. Nimbus Cloud Services, one of the listed competitors, approaches the company with a compelling acquisition offer at a significant premium. The offer would provide liquidity to employees and investors while securing the company's technology future.

The Fallout: The board unanimously supports entering exclusive negotiations, but under the side letter, TeleComet's consent is required. Acting on instructions from its parent company, TeleComet exercises its veto right. The deal collapses before definitive documents are signed. Word of the failed transaction spreads informally among potential acquirers, who conclude that SecureLayer cannot be sold to the most motivated buyers. Competing offers evaporate, and the company's valuation momentum fades.

Positive Scenario: The Constructive Transition

The Setup: HealthLink AI, a startup building patient-data interoperability software, raises a strategic Series B investment from MedNova Ventures, the CVC arm of a midsize regional medical device company. The side letter includes a change-of-control clause stating that if HealthLink is acquired by a competitor of MedNova, all joint pilot programs and data-integration projects will automatically terminate, with each party deleting shared data and returning confidential materials. No consent or veto rights are included.

The Interaction: Two years later, MedSphere Global, one of the largest healthcare IT firms in the world, approaches HealthLink with an acquisition offer. The deal promises global reach, deeper technical resources, and an opportunity to embed HealthLink's technology across thousands of hospitals. Because MedSphere competes directly with MedNova, the change-of-control clause is triggered. HealthLink notifies MedNova, the pilots wind down smoothly, and data connections are severed within the contractual 60-day window.

The Outcome: The transaction proceeds without dispute. MedNova's commercial exposure is contained, its confidential data is protected, and the startup's new parent gains an expanded market footprint. Post-acquisition, MedSphere integrates HealthLink deeply into their systems, vastly increasing its impact, and eventually opens it up so competitors, including MedNova, can license the technology. Despite acquisition by a competitor, the relationship remained professional and intact.

Founder's Takeaway: When narrowly defined and limited to operational matters, a change-of-control provision can serve as a practical safeguard rather than a constraint. By avoiding veto or consent rights and focusing only on partnership termination and data separation, founders can reassure corporate investors that their strategic interests are protected while preserving full freedom to pursue transformative opportunities.

Deal Term: Joint Development Agreements

Mechanics: Joint Development Agreements (JDAs) are a powerful tool to help align a startup with a large corporation, and are often the key strategic rationale for a CVC investing. A side letter may include a clause committing the startup and the CVC's parent company to negotiate a JDA "in good faith" following the close of the investment. This is distinct from, and far preferable to, a side letter that attempts to dictate the specific technical and commercial terms of the JDA itself. A "good faith" clause creates a legal obligation for both parties to seriously and honestly attempt to reach a deal, but it does not bind them to the specific terms, allowing for a proper, arms-length negotiation.

CVC Motivation: For the CVC, securing a commitment to negotiate a JDA is a way to formalize the path toward a strategic collaboration, which is often the core of their investment thesis. It allows the CVC investor to demonstrate to their internal stakeholders, including business units and executive leadership, that the investment is not just a financial bet but has a tangible pathway to delivering strategic value. This signal of intent can be crucial for getting the investment approved internally and for justifying the CVC's existence and budget.

Implications for a Startup: A side letter clause committing to negotiate a JDA can be a powerful positive signal to other investors in the round. It suggests that a major corporate player has not only validated your technology enough to invest, but also sees a clear path to becoming a paying development partner or customer, which de-risks your commercial roadmap. However, the primary danger lies in how this JDA is structured and paid for. A CVC may attempt to "pay" for the JDA with the equity from the financing round, a toxic arrangement that conflates investment with revenue. A JDA and an equity investment should **always** be separate transactions. Development work should be paid for in cash, ensuring a clean valuation and a clear separation of your roles as a portfolio company and a vendor.

Positive Scenario: The Non-Dilutive Catalyst

The Setup: PharmaLeap, a startup with a proprietary AI platform for identifying novel drug targets, is raising its Series A. They attract interest from Global Health Ventures, the CVC arm of a top-ten pharmaceutical company. Global Health's investment is contingent on a side letter that includes a commitment for both parties to "negotiate in good faith a separate, cash-paid Joint Development Agreement within six months of closing."

The Interaction: The Series A closes with the side letter in place. The CVC's internal champion immediately facilitates high-level meetings between PharmaLeap's scientific founders and the head of R&D for the parent's oncology division. Because the *intent* to partner is already contractually established, the conversations are highly productive, focusing on the "how" rather than the "if." They quickly scope out a project to apply PharmaLeap's platform to a specific set of difficult-to-kill cancer targets from the parent's pipeline.

The Outcome: Just three months after the investment, PharmaLeap signs a $2 million, 18-month JDA with the CVC's parent company. This agreement is paid in cash over installments based on progress, providing PharmaLeap with a significant stream of non-dilutive revenue. More importantly, the JDA gives them access to the parent's proprietary biological data, which they use to train and validate their AI models, dramatically enhancing their platform's capabilities. When PharmaLeap goes to raise its Series B, they can show not only strong technical progress but also a multi-million-dollar commercial contract with a global pharma leader, leading to a highly competitive round at a substantial step-up in valuation.

Negative Scenario: The Equity-Funded R&D Trap

The Setup: FusionCore, a startup developing a novel liquid cooling system for high-performance data centers, is raising a $5 million seed round. They get a term sheet from ServerWorks Capital, the CVC of a large server hardware manufacturer. The side letter, however, contains a clause stating that in exchange for the investment, FusionCore will "dedicate sufficient engineering resources to a joint development project to integrate and optimize its technology for ServerWorks' next-generation server architecture," with the scope of work detailed in a lengthy appendix. There is no mention of any cash payment for this work.

The Negotiation: The FusionCore founders are thrilled at the prospect of being designed into ServerWorks' new product line. The CVC frames the arrangement as a "deeply strategic partnership," and the founders, focused on the $5 million headline investment number, agree. They rationalize that this is their path to market.

The Fallout

1. **Conflated Value**: The investment closes. The JDA begins immediately, and it quickly becomes a massive engineering effort. The project requires the full-time attention of half of FusionCore's engineering team for over a year. They are, in effect, performing outsourced R&D for ServerWorks, paid for with their own equity.
2. **Effective Valuation Hit**: The founders soon realize that a significant portion of their seed funding is not being used to grow their business, but to subsidize the development costs of their new investor. Their effective investment was not $5 million, but perhaps only half of that, with the rest being "revenue" that they paid for with a huge chunk of their company. Their effective fundraising and valuation were drastically lower than they thought.
3. **Loss of Leverage**: When FusionCore tries to engage with other potential server manufacturers, they are met with resistance. Other CVCs ask for similar terms to ServerWorks, but these JDAs are no longer financially viable for FusionCore. They also have much less runway than they anticipated, because much of the "fundraise" had to be spent to pay for their JDA work.

Founder's Takeaway: A JDA can be a company-making opportunity, but it must be a commercial transaction, not an investment term. A commitment to *negotiate* a JDA in a side letter is a positive signal. A side letter that *is* the JDA, paid for with your own equity, is a commitment to months of unpaid work when your team could be more productively focused on revenue-generating opportunities elsewhere. Always insist on separating the investment from any commercial agreements and ensure that any development work you perform for a partner is compensated at a fair market rate.

Deal Term: "Major Investor" Information Rights

Mechanics: This term contractually obligates the startup to provide the CVC with standard financial statements on a regular basis, typically within 30–45 days of each quarter's end. These financials almost always include the three core statements: the Balance Sheet (a snapshot of assets and liabilities), the Income Statement (also known as the P&L, showing revenues and expenses), and the Statement of Cash Flows. While this right is a standard component of the main IRA for investors who meet a certain "Major Investor" threshold, a CVC may request it in a side letter if they are a smaller investor in the round or if their parent has specific formatting or compliance requirements.

CVC Motivation: The CVC's parent company, especially if it is a publicly traded entity, operates under a complex web of financial reporting obligations. Accounting standards (like ASC 321 and IFRS 9) require them to value their equity investments and report on their performance to their own auditors, shareholders, and regulatory bodies like the Securities and Exchange Commission (SEC). This information right is not typically sought for strategic intelligence or micromanagement; it is a fundamental compliance requirement for their own finance and accounting departments.

Implications for a Startup: This is a low-risk and, in almost all cases, a net-positive provision. Agreeing to this is a simple way to build goodwill and demonstrate professionalism. More importantly, it imposes a healthy discipline on a startup's internal financial reporting cadence. The process of generating clean, accurate, and timely financial statements forces a level of operational rigor that is a best practice for any well-run company, regardless of its investors.

Founder's Takeaway: View standard information rights not as a burdensome obligation, but as a necessary cost of business. The discipline it imposes will pay dividends in improved operational decision-making, stronger investor relationships, and a smoother, more successful fundraising process for every subsequent round.

Deal Term: Management Access

Mechanics: This clause formalizes an obligation for the startup's management team to meet regularly with representatives from the CVC parent company's strategic, operational, R&D, or corporate development teams. The cadence and format can range from vaguely defined "periodic meetings" to a more structured "quarterly strategic review with the business unit leadership." Unlike a board or observer seat, this right does not grant access to the company's formal governance process but creates a direct, operational channel between the startup's leadership and the corporate parent.

CVC Motivation: For the CVC, management access is a powerful tool for value creation and monitoring. It facilitates deep knowledge transfer, allows the parent's business units to explore and de-risk partnership opportunities more effectively, and keeps the startup "top-of-mind" within the vast corporate structure, ensuring strategic projects don't fall through the cracks. It also serves as a hedge against the risk that a particularly "hot" startup, flush with new capital, might de-prioritize a strategic collaboration in favor of other customers; regular meetings keep the partnership on the agenda.

Implications for a Startup: This can be a significant boon for startups genuinely seeking a deep strategic partnership. Direct, regular access to the parent company's decision-makers can dramatically accelerate joint development, shorten sales cycles, and provide an invaluable feedback loop. The primary risk from this clause is the immense and often underestimated time commitment. "Death by a thousand meetings" is a real danger that can pull a CEO and senior leadership away from their core duties of building the product and running the company.

It is often better to keep these arrangements as informal "handshake agreements." Proactively setting up a recurring meeting on the calendar before the side letter is even negotiated can be a great way to demonstrate commitment and alleviate the corporate's concerns without being contractually obligated. If the term must be formalized, keep the obligations vague (e.g., "periodic meetings at a mutually agreed time"), allow for other team members (like a Head of Partnerships or a technical lead) to attend instead of the CEO, and ensure the startup has the right to set the agenda.

Positive Scenario: The Co-Creation Cadence

The Setup: An enterprise AI startup, "SynthLogic," which has a platform for optimizing manufacturing processes, takes a Series A investment from "AutoCorp Ventures," the CVC of a global automotive manufacturer. The side letter includes a "mutual agreement to hold quarterly deep-dive sessions" between SynthLogic's product team and AutoCorp's head of factory automation.

The Interaction: The meetings become a highly productive, co-creative working session. In the first meeting, SynthLogic presents its product roadmap. The AutoCorp team provides invaluable feedback, highlighting two features that are "nice-to-have" but pointing to a third, unplanned feature as a "must-have" that would unlock a massive budget: predictive maintenance scheduling based on robotic arm telemetry.

The Outcome: SynthLogic adjusts its roadmap, prioritizing the predictive maintenance feature. The quarterly meetings become a rapid feedback loop, with AutoCorp's engineers providing real-world data and insights that allow SynthLogic to build a far more robust and valuable product. Nine months later, AutoCorp signs a multi-million dollar, multi-year contract to deploy the new module across its global network of factories. The management access clause was the catalyst for a deep partnership that shaped the product and secured a cornerstone customer. SynthLogic continues work on its other "nice-to-have" features, but uses the robot arm product as its entry point into other automotive and manufacturing companies.

Negative Scenario: Death by a Thousand Meetings

The Setup: A cybersecurity startup, "SecurAll," takes an investment from a massive, diversified tech conglomerate, "MegaCorp." The CVC, under pressure to show "synergy," insists on a side letter term requiring "monthly update meetings between SecurAll CEO and CTO with any interested MegaCorp business unit." The founders, eager to please, agree.

The Interaction: The reality is a nightmare. The SecurAll Chief Executive Officer (CEO) and Chief Technology Officer (CTO) find their calendars swamped. One month, they're meeting with MegaCorp's cloud division. Next, it's the e-commerce team, then the hardware group, then the international sales team. Each meeting requires a custom presentation and a re-explanation of their technology from first principles to a new group of people, most of whom have no budget or real intent to partner, just to learn and build market intelligence. They try to pass this meeting off to their sales team, but MegaCorp views this as a slight and insists on the contractual obligation of the CEO and CTO to give the presentations.

The Fallout

1 **Massive Time Sink**: The CEO and CTO are spending nearly a quarter of their time preparing for and attending these internal MegaCorp meetings. This is the time they are not spending on product development, hiring, or talking to actual paying customers.
2 **Execution Grinds to a Halt**: The distraction has a direct impact on the company's velocity. The launch of their V2 product is delayed by a full quarter. Their lead over smaller, more focused competitors begins to erode.
3 **Strategic Whiplash**: Each MegaCorp division has a different "ask," pulling the startup in multiple directions. The cloud team wants a specific integration, while the hardware team wants them to explore an entirely different use case. The startup is caught in a cycle of strategic whiplash, unable to focus on a coherent roadmap. By the time they go to raise their next round, their growth has stalled, and new investors are concerned about their lack of focus.

Founder's Takeaway: Management access can provide a valuable bridge to a corporate partner, but that bridge must have a clear purpose and a well-defined traffic controller. Vague, open-ended access rights are a recipe for distraction and strategic chaos. Always negotiate to control the cadence, the agenda, and the attendees of these meetings, ensuring that every hour spent with your corporate partner is a high-leverage activity that drives your business forward, rather than a low-value obligation that holds it back. Make sure that you can delegate meeting responsibilities away from the founder and CEO to a sales or corporate development employee, as necessary. Best of all, proactively set up regularly scheduled recurring meetings so that the CVC does not feel pressure to impose this term at all.

Deal Term: Publicity and Announcement Rights

Mechanics: This term grants the CVC and its parent corporation the right to review, approve, and often co-author any public communications that mention the investment, the partnership, or the parent company's brand. The scope typically covers press releases, blog posts, social media announcements, and sometimes even website content that mentions the CVC or the parent company. The process usually requires the startup to submit a draft announcement for review by the CVC's corporate communications and legal departments, who may suggest edits or require changes before granting approval.

CVC Motivation: For a large corporation, brand management is a critical function. Their primary motivation is to maintain strict control over their corporate brand, public messaging, and narrative. Any external communication must align with their established brand guidelines, strategic messaging, and legal disclosure requirements. This review process prevents inaccurate or off-brand statements and ensures that the announcement of the investment is framed in a way that benefits the parent company's image as an innovator.

Implications for a Startup: This is a standard and generally low-risk term that founders should expect and even welcome. The primary downside is a potential delay in announcements; a large corporation's internal review process can be bureaucratic and slow, sometimes taking several weeks. However, the potential upside is enormous, as it allows the startup to leverage the CVC parent's powerful PR machine, established media relationships, and brand credibility to amplify its own message.

Positive Scenario: The CodeSentry Launchpad

The Setup: CodeSentry, a B2B startup with a groundbreaking AI platform for real-time code security analysis, has just closed its $10 million Series

A. The round was led by a respected institutional VC, and CodeSentry's founders successfully negotiated a strategic allocation from Titan Software Ventures, the CVC arm of a global enterprise software giant. The side letter includes a standard clause for joint approval of all publicity and announcements mentioning Titan Software.

The Process: Instead of a simple funding announcement, the CodeSentry CEO works proactively with the CVC's marketing lead. They draft a press release that focuses not just on the capital raised, but on the *strategic partnership* with Titan Software. The draft is sent to Titan's corporate communications team. Instead of just a simple sign-off, Titan's team sees an opportunity. They re-craft the narrative, positioning CodeSentry not just as a portfolio company, but as a key innovator in the future of secure software development, a major strategic priority for Titan. The final output is a polished, co-branded press release featuring a powerful quote from Titan Software's Chief Technology Officer on how CodeSentry is revolutionizing its code security.

The Fallout

1 **Tier-1 Media Amplification:** The announcement is not just posted on a wire service; it's actively pushed by Titan Software's PR agency to their network of contacts at top-tier technology and business publications. The story gets picked up by major outlets that would have never covered a standard Series A announcement from a small startup.
2 **Explosion in High-Quality Inbound Leads:** The morning the press release goes live, CodeSentry's website is flooded with traffic. More importantly, the traffic is from the right people. Instead of small businesses and individual developers, they see demo requests pouring in from Chief Information Security Officers (CISOs) and VPs of Engineering at Fortune 500 companies, the exact enterprise customers they had been struggling to get meetings with. These high-level execs *need* to talk with CodeSentry and be aware of what they do, in case their bosses read the news about Titan Software and ask, "are we speaking with CodeSentry too?" The validation from the Titan Software brand acted as the ultimate seal of approval and a funnel for inbound sales requests.
3 **A Magnet for Top Talent:** The high-profile coverage positions CodeSentry as a leader in its field. Elite AI and cybersecurity engineers, who would typically only consider working at a large tech giant, begin actively applying for roles, drawn by the opportunity to work at a nimble startup that has the backing and credibility of a major industry player (and therefore, are taking much less of a career risk by moving).
4 **Ecosystem Validation:** The announcement does more than attract customers and talent; it establishes CodeSentry as a pillar in the developer

tool ecosystem. Other companies in the space begin reaching out to discuss potential integration partnerships, further entrenching CodeSentry's platform in the market.

Founder's Takeaway: Although publicity and announcement rights are a bureaucratic hurdle that can be frustrating to a startup that wants to move fast, they are also a strategic opportunity. Instead of passively waiting for approval, founders should actively collaborate with their CVC partner's communications team and provide them with a compelling narrative, high-quality assets (logos, founder headshots, product screenshots), and a clear message. By making it easy for them to tell a great story, you can transform a simple funding announcement into a powerful go-to-market event that generates immediate and lasting value for your company.

Deal Term: Right of First Offer/Right of First Refusal on Acquisition

Mechanics: These two rights, while often discussed together, function differently but have a similar chilling effect on a startup's M&A prospects.

- **A Right of First Offer (ROFO)** requires the startup, should it decide to pursue a sale, to first approach the CVC's parent and negotiate exclusively with them for a defined period (e.g., 30–60 days) before engaging in M&A discussions with any other party. Notably, it does not grant the parent company the right to see the price or terms of their competitor's final bid.
- **A Right of First Refusal (ROFR)** is more potent. It grants the CVC's parent the right to match any bona fide third-party acquisition offer that the startup's board intends to accept.

CVC Motivation: The motivation is twofold: offensive and defensive. Offensively, it ensures the parent company has a privileged "option" to acquire a startup if it becomes a highly valuable strategic asset. Defensively, and often more importantly, it grants the parent the power to block a competitor from acquiring a key technology or market position by simply matching the offer themselves. It is a powerful tool for controlling the startup's ultimate destiny.

Implications for a Startup: While at first glance these terms might seem to create a "bidding war," they almost always do the opposite. Potential acquirers are extremely unwilling to act as a "stalking horse," investing hundreds of hours and millions of dollars in legal and financial due diligence to arrive at a price, only to have that work handed on a silver platter to a CVC parent who can match the offer without any of the upfront risk or effort. The existence of a ROFO or ROFR must be disclosed early in any M&A process, and for many financially motivated acquirers, it is an immediate deal-killer. This prevents a competitive auction from ever materializing, which can lead to a significantly lower acquisition price. These terms should be avoided unless the CVC's parent is unequivocally the most likely, most strategic, and most desirable acquirer for your company.

Negative Scenario: The Chilled Auction

The Setup: ConnectAI, a startup with a breakthrough AI-powered customer service platform, is gaining significant traction in the enterprise market. In their Series A, they took an investment from Legacy Systems Ventures, the CVC of a slow-moving, incumbent enterprise software giant, LegacySys. The side letter included a ROFR on any acquisition.

The Interaction: Two years later, ConnectAI's board decides the time is right to explore an acquisition and hires an investment bank to run a competitive process. The bankers identify several logical buyers, with the most enthusiastic being InnovateCloud, a fast-growing competitor to LegacySys. InnovateCloud's corporate development team is highly motivated, seeing ConnectAI as the perfect acquisition to cement their market leadership. They sign an NDA and are granted access to the data room to begin preliminary diligence.

The Fallout

1 **The Discovery**: Within days, InnovateCloud's legal team reviews the key financing documents in the data room and discovers the ROFR held by their chief rival, LegacySys. The M&A team immediately flags it to their executive leadership.
2 **The Strategic Withdrawal**: The InnovateCloud executives hold an emergency meeting. The head of corporate development lays out the situation bluntly: "We believe this company is worth at least $500 million. But if we spend the next three months and $2 million on diligence to prove that value and make an offer, LegacySys can just sit back, wait for us to do all the work, and then match our price. We would be acting as their free M&A department. We are not going to be their stalking horse." InnovateCloud formally withdraws from the process, citing the unacceptable M&A risk created by the ROFR.
3 **The Market is Chilled**: ConnectAI's investment bankers approach other potential buyers, but the story is the same. Once the ROFR is disclosed, the most aggressive bidders walk away, unwilling to set the price for LegacySys. The competitive auction collapses before it ever begins. ConnectAI is left with only one serious suitor: LegacySys, who,

knowing they have no competition, submits a low, take-it-or-leave-it offer of $350 million. The board, facing limited options, is forced to accept.

Founder's Takeaway: ROFO and ROFR are not tools for creating a bidding war; they are tools for preventing one. Their true danger is not that a great offer will be matched, but that the best offers will never be made in the first place. By granting a ROFO or ROFR, you are signaling to the market that you are not running a fair and open process, which can dramatically limit your options and reduce your company's ultimate exit value. These terms should be avoided unless your investor is clearly the most likely and best potential acquirer of your startup.

Deal Term: ROFO/ROFR/MFN on Partnerships or Technology

Mechanics: These terms grant the CVC's parent company preferential rights regarding the startup's commercial and strategic partnerships.

- An **MFN** clause is the most common and least restrictive. It ensures that the CVC's parent will receive terms (e.g., pricing, features) that are at least as favorable as those granted to any of its competitors. This right can be granted indefinitely or for a limited period of time.
- A **ROFO** on partnerships requires the startup to negotiate exclusively with the CVC parent for a set period before engaging with a competitor on a similar commercial deal.
- A **ROFR** on partnerships is the most restrictive. It grants the parent the right to match the terms of any partnership deal the startup strikes with a competitor, effectively taking the deal for themselves. This term is quite rare.

CVC Motivation: The primary goal is to secure preferential access to the startup's technology and prevent key competitors from gaining a strategic advantage. An MFN protects them from being disadvantaged, while ROFOs and ROFRs are offensive tools to capture or control valuable partnerships before rivals can, especially in situations where a startup can only have one logical partner per geography.

Implications for a Startup: An MFN is often a reasonable and even beneficial request if the parent company is a key anchor customer, as it solidifies the relationship. However, ROFOs and ROFRs on partnerships are highly problematic. They create a significant chilling effect on other potential partners, who will be reluctant to invest the time and legal fees to negotiate a deal, knowing that the CVC's parent can swoop in and take it at the last minute. This can stifle a startup's business development efforts and limit its ability to form a broad ecosystem of partners.

Positive Scenario: The MFN Anchor

The Setup: ComponentCo, a startup that has developed a more efficient power transformer for industrial electric motors, takes a Series A investment from an Industrial Conglomerate's CVC, "Industrial Ventures." The parent, a major motor manufacturer, is ComponentCo's first large customer. The side letter includes an MFN clause on pricing for the next five years.

The Interaction: The partnership is a success, and ComponentCo's transformers help Industrial Conglomerate launch a best-in-class, energy-efficient motor. A year later, a smaller competitor approaches ComponentCo and, in an effort to catch up, offers to pay a 10% premium for the same transformers.

The Outcome: ComponentCo is able to use the competitor's offer to their advantage. They inform Industrial Ventures of the new pricing, which they will use as an anchor for their next negotiation with Industrial Conglomerate. The MFN has served its purpose: it allowed the Industrial Conglomerate to feel secure as an early partner, while still allowing ComponentCo to benefit from market-based price discovery. The relationship is strengthened (Industrial Conglomerate believes they got a good deal), and the startup's financials improve.

Negative Scenario: The Supply Chain Poison Pill

The Setup: A startup, "Advanced Composites," develops a revolutionary, lightweight material that is perfect for next-generation aircraft. They take an investment from "AeroCorp Ventures," the CVC of a large, established aerospace manufacturer. The side letter includes a ROFR on any major supply or partnership agreements. Advanced Composites has only one factory and limited production capacity.

The Interaction: An innovative electric aircraft company, "E-Wing," wants to build its new flagship jet around Advanced Composites' material. They propose a massive, multi-year, exclusive supply agreement that would make Advanced Composites' business double overnight and absorb 80% of their production capacity. This deal would put E-Wing years ahead of its competitor, AeroCorp.

The Fallout

1 **The Chilling Disclosure**: As negotiations advance, Advanced Composites is forced to disclose the ROFR held by AeroCorp. The E-Wing executive team immediately grasps the catastrophic strategic risk.
2 **The Competitor Control Problem**: E-Wing's COO explains the danger: "If we sign this deal, AeroCorp can then simply exercise their ROFR, match the terms, and take the deal for themselves. Advanced Composites doesn't have the capacity to serve both of us, and Aerocorp would

instantly control the supply of the most critical component for our new aircraft, starving us of the materials we need to compete with them. We need a supply chain that we know will be reliable, and we cannot allow our direct rival to have that kind of power over our manufacturing capacity."

3 **The Ideal Partner Walks**: Despite the superiority of the material, E-Wing's board cannot approve a strategy that places their production at the mercy of their biggest competitor. They reluctantly walk away from the deal and are forced to design their new aircraft around a competing nascent material. Advanced Composites loses its company-making contract because of the ROFR, and worse, is sending revenue-generating opportunities to its competitors who will try to emulate Advanced Composites' materials.

Founder's Takeaway: Partnership rights require a careful balancing act. An MFN clause can be a smart way to solidify a relationship with a key anchor customer, turning their investment into a long-term commitment. However, ROFO and ROFR on partnerships can be much more dangerous when you are limited in your capacity to sell or implement your product (such as being limited in integration engineers or manufacturing capacity). Fortunately, these dangers are much less pronounced in software or companies that can inexpensively ramp up production. Always evaluate these terms based on their potential to either catalyze or constrain your business development efforts.

Deal Term: Technology Licensing

Mechanics: This term, typically found in a side letter, grants the CVC's parent company a license to use the startup's technology. The scope of this license can vary dramatically, from a narrow, time-bound license for internal R&D purposes only, to a broad, perpetual, worldwide, royalty-free license to use the startup's core technology in the parent's commercial products. The specifics of the license, its scope, duration, exclusivity, and financial terms (or lack thereof), are the most critical elements. Like with JDAs, it is best practice for the side letter to oblige both sides to negotiate a technology licensing deal "in good faith" through a separate agreement.

CVC Motivation: From the CVC's perspective, securing a technology license is one of the most direct ways to deliver strategic value back to the parent corporation. It provides the parent with immediate access to the startup's core innovation, which can be used to accelerate its own product development, enhance existing offerings, or explore new markets. A preferential or royalty-free license is seen as a tangible, quantifiable strategic return on the investment, separate from any future financial exit.

Implications for a Startup: This can be a great boon to the startup, validating the importance of its technology, but if negotiated poorly, it can be contentious and potentially hazardous. A broad, royalty-free license to your core technology can be equivalent to giving away your product for free to a major potential customer, completely undermining your business model and potentially even your ability to sell to others. However, a narrowly defined (in both duration and scope) and properly compensated license can be the foundation of a powerful commercial partnership. The cardinal rule for founders is that any technology license should be treated as a separate commercial agreement, negotiated at arm's length with market-rate royalties or fees, even if its principles are outlined in a side letter. It is best to include the technology in a separate document, with the side letter to state that the startup and CVC will "negotiate in good faith" toward reaching a technology license agreement.

Positive Scenario: The Win-Win Partnership

The Setup: OpsLogic is a SaaS startup that sells a sophisticated AI-powered platform for managing complex manufacturing supply chains. To build this platform, their internal DevOps team created a brilliant, proprietary tool for monitoring and optimizing cloud infrastructure costs in real-time. This tool is a powerful internal asset but is not their core product, and they have no plans to commercialize it. OpsLogic takes a Series A investment from EnterpriseSoftware Ventures, the CVC of a massive software conglomerate that spends hundreds of millions on cloud hosting annually.

The Negotiation: During diligence, the CVC team is impressed not only by the core supply chain product but also by the internal cloud-cost optimization tool. They recognize its immense value to their parent company. In the side letter, they include a commitment to negotiate in good faith a commercial license for this *specific internal tool*. The key is that this is negotiated as a separate, parallel agreement, for the tool to be used only internally.

The Outcome: The final agreement is a win-win. OpsLogic receives its equity investment from the CVC. Shortly afterwards, the parent company signs a three-year, seven-figure commercial licensing agreement to use OpsLogic's cloud-cost optimization tool.

1 **Non-Dilutive Revenue**: OpsLogic secures a major stream of non-dilutive revenue for a non-core asset, strengthening its balance sheet and extending its runway.
2 **Marquee Customer Validation**: They land one of the world's largest software companies as a paying customer, providing a powerful validation point for future sales and fundraising.

3 **Strategic Alignment**: The parent company receives significant value, making the CVC look like heroes internally and strengthening their commitment to OpsLogic's long-term success.

This scenario works because the licensed technology was not the core product being sold to the broader market, can only be used internally (the corporate cannot resell the tech to compete with OpsLogic), and the license was treated as a distinct, paid commercial transaction.

Negative Scenario: The SecureComms Giveaway

The Setup: SecureComms, a cybersecurity startup, has developed a revolutionary end-to-end encryption algorithm for enterprise messaging. They are raising a seed round and are excited to receive a term sheet from CommGiant Ventures, the CVC of a global telecommunications and enterprise software company. Buried in the side letter is a clause granting the parent company a "perpetual, irrevocable, worldwide, royalty-free, non-exclusive license" to use the SecureComms algorithm and incorporate it into any of its current and future products.

The Negotiation: The SecureComms founders are a technical team, inexperienced in fundraising. They are so focused on the validation that comes with the CommGiant brand and the size of the investment check that they don't fully appreciate the implications of the license. Their lawyers raise a red flag, but the CVC assures them it's a "standard term for a strategic investment" and is non-negotiable. Eager to close the round, the founders agree.

The Fallout

1 **Business Model Blunted**: Six months after the deal closes, CommGiant launches a new version of its flagship enterprise messaging suite, which now includes "military-grade encryption" powered by SecureComms' algorithm, as a free upgrade for all its customers. SecureComms' primary value proposition has just been given away for free by its largest potential collaborator.
2 **Market Precluded**: When the SecureComms' sales team tries to sell their product to other large enterprises, they are repeatedly shut down. Potential customers ask, "Why would we pay you for this feature when we already get it for free from CommGiant, our primary software vendor?"
3 **Un-investable Company**: A year later, SecureComms is struggling to generate revenue and tries to raise a Series A. New investors immediately balk during due diligence when they discover the royalty-free license. They rightly conclude that the company has given away its

crown jewels and has no viable path to building a large, independent business.

4 **Acqui-hire or Failure**: With no path to revenue and no ability to raise follow-on funding, SecureComms is left with two options: be "acqui-hired" by CommGiant for a fraction of its potential value (essentially a talent acquisition) or shut down entirely.

Founder's Takeaway: A broad, royalty-free license for your core technology is an existential threat. It is almost never a standard term and should be treated as a deal-breaker. If a CVC insists on a license as a condition of investment, the negotiation must pivot to treating it as a commercial deal. The best approach is to replace the license clause in the side letter with a simple "agreement to negotiate a commercial licensing agreement in good faith" as a separate workstream. This cleanly separates the equity investment from the commercial partnership, allowing you to negotiate a fair market price for your product, just as you would with any other customer and ensures that the commercial partnership can stand on its own.

Best Practices

Most corporate venture capital side letters rely on familiar mechanisms: information rights, major investor rights, and board observers that mirror standard venture practices with only slight variations in scope or intent. These are the predictable elements of a CVC partnership. These terms create visibility, coordination, and accountability between the startup and the investor. When negotiated carefully, they rarely alter the company's long-term trajectory. Key strategic terms, like a technology license or a JDA, reinforce why the CVC was interested in working with you in the first place, and are usually mutually beneficial agreements. It is best to negotiate these commercial terms separately from the side letter, but a commitment in the side letter *to* negotiate these terms can help speed up the commercial process.

Yet, beyond this well-traveled terrain lie provisions that are far less routine. Some emerge from a corporation's legal or regulatory constraints, others reflect strategic motives that simply do not exist in financial VC. These uncommon terms, such as early redemption rights, IP rights, and access to operational metrics, carry asymmetrical consequences if misunderstood. They are not inherently predatory, but they can reshape control, exit flexibility, or valuation in ways founders do not anticipate. The next chapter examines these non-standard terms, explaining why they appear, what risks they introduce, and how a founder can negotiate them without closing the door on strategic partnership.

Exhibit 5.1 A table comparing relatively common terms in CVC side letters

Term	*Impact*	*Comments*
Assignment rights	Low	Permit intragroup transfers only; block assignments outside the corporate family
Board observer rights	Low–medium	Allow exclusion for conflicts and sensitive topics or suggest management access instead
Carve-outs from non-compete agreements	Low	Usually non-negotiable and with limited downside
Change-of-control provisions—change of control of startup	Low–high	Operational termination/ data-wind-down rights are fine; avoid consent/veto mechanics that restrict exits
Joint development agreements	Medium	Useful when paid and scoped; keep JDA separate from equity terms and define IP/exit ramps
Major investor information rights	Low	Usually non-negotiable and with limited downside, good practice for future fundraising
Management access	Low–medium	Best to proactively set meetings so this term is not brought up. Otherwise, allow for non-senior members to take meetings
Publicity and announcement rights	Low	Use this to your advantage to leverage the parent company's PR teams
ROFO/ROFR on acquisition	High	Can chill acquisition talks. Avoid unless CVC parent is your clear best buyer
ROFO/ROFR/MFN on partnerships or technology	Medium	Keep to defined products, short/ constrained terms, and precise notice mechanics
Technology licensing	Medium	Separate commercial license from equity; ensure fair market terms and no "free" rights tied to investment

Chapter 6

Less Common CVC Terms

Now that we have established a foundation in the more common provisions found in corporate venture transactions, it is time to turn to the less familiar territory. The following terms appear less frequently but can carry outsized strategic or legal implications when they do. These provisions often arise from a corporation's unique operational constraints or competitive concerns, and while they are not inherently unfavorable, they demand closer scrutiny. Understanding how and why these uncommon terms surface will help founders anticipate negotiation dynamics and preserve flexibility as partnerships deepen.

Deal Term: Carve-Outs from Drag-Along Provisions

Mechanics: A standard and critical provision in any venture financing is the "drag-along" right, typically found in the voting agreement. This right allows a majority of shareholders (or a specific majority of preferred shareholders) to "drag along" all other minority shareholders, forcing them to sell their shares and approve an acquisition of the company. A corporate venture capital (CVC) may use a side letter to negotiate a carve-out that exempts them from this drag-along obligation, giving them the right to refuse to sell their shares in a transaction approved by all other investors. This carve-out is often specifically triggered if the potential acquirer is a named competitor of the CVC's parent company.

CVC Motivation: The CVC's motivation is to prevent a scenario where it is contractually forced to aid a direct competitor of its parent company. An acquisition of a portfolio company by a rival could transfer valuable technology, talent, and market position to that rival. In this situation, the CVC's parent company cannot abide by a situation where its own investment capital is used to facilitate a strategic win for its competition. The carve-out serves as an absolute backstop to prevent this from happening.

Implications for a Startup: While the CVC's motivation is understandable, this carve-out can be a deal-breaker for a potential acquirer and

DOI: 10.4324/9781003758280-7

introduces significant M&A risk for the startup. An acquirer's goal is almost always to own 100% of the target company to ensure full control and a clean corporate structure. The presence of a single, uncooperative minority shareholder can be an insurmountable obstacle, causing the acquirer to walk away from the deal entirely. If that shareholder were a member of the board, they would be in violation of their fiduciary duties. This provision should be avoided if at all possible. (Note that having a CVC on the board does not protect you from this clause, as the director could resign immediately before triggering these carve-out provisions.) Effectively, this gives a CVC a "super-preferred" share that gives them rights no other investor class has, and may scare off future investment, not just acquisition offers, for the company.

Negative Scenario: The DataWeave Deadlock

The Setup: DataWeave, a fast-growing startup building a groundbreaking platform for real-time data analytics, raises a $60 million Series C round. Among the new investors is CloudGiant Ventures, the corporate venture arm of CloudGiant, one of the world's largest public cloud providers. As part of the deal, CloudGiant negotiates a side letter granting it special rights and protections. One clause provides a carve-out from the company's drag-along provision. Specifically, CloudGiant Ventures is exempt from being forced to sell its shares in any acquisition by a "named list of competitors," which includes the top five hyperscale cloud and enterprise software players. At the time, this seems harmless; the founders view it as a standard competitive safeguard.

The Acquisition Offer: Two years later, DataWeave's technology becomes the industry standard for enterprise data synchronization. The company receives a blockbuster acquisition offer from InfraScale, a Fortune 100 enterprise software company and direct rival to CloudGiant in the cloud database market. The offer values DataWeave at over ten times its last valuation. The board votes unanimously to accept, and a supermajority of shareholders approve the deal. With diligence complete and signatures imminent, the entire company prepares for an exit that will cement DataWeave as one of the decade's biggest success stories.

The Conflict: During final negotiations, InfraScale's legal team reviews the capitalization table and notices the carve-out in CloudGiant Ventures' side letter. When InfraScale's counsel requests confirmation that all shareholders will tender their shares, CloudGiant Ventures formally notifies the board that it is invoking its drag-along carve-out and will not sell its 5% stake. This means CloudGiant, InfraScale's fiercest competitor, would remain a minority shareholder in InfraScale's new, wholly owned subsidiary after the merger. InfraScale's CEO immediately balks. From a strategic and operational standpoint, allowing a rival access to sensitive customer and technical information is unacceptable.

The Fallout

1 **Deal Collapse:** InfraScale's board issues an ultimatum: either CloudGiant's shares are included in the sale, or the deal is off. CloudGiant refuses to budge, citing its contractual rights under the side letter. With no legal mechanism to compel the sale of those shares, the transaction collapses just days before closing. The news leaks, sending shockwaves through the startup ecosystem.
2 **Reputational Damage:** The failed acquisition becomes public, and DataWeave is suddenly viewed as "unacquirable" by any of Cloud Giant's competitors. What once looked like a strategic endorsement from a top-tier CVC now appears to be a poison pill that deters every logical acquirer in its space.
3 **Internal and External Conflict:** The institutional VCs and early backers are furious. Board members argue that CloudGiant's unilateral action has vaporized hundreds of millions of dollars of paper gains and destroyed years of value creation. Board meetings devolve into finger-pointing and recrimination, with investors questioning how such a provision was ever approved. Legal counsel begins exploring whether the CVC breached its duties or acted in bad faith, a complex and uncertain battle.
4 **Severely Limited Exit Options:** With its most attractive buyer off the table, DataWeave's strategic exit paths have been dramatically reduced. Potential acquirers fear similar complications, while CloudGiant's competitors refuse to engage. The company is left with two difficult options: pursue a lower-valuation sale to a non-competitive buyer, such as a private equity firm, or attempt a risky IPO. Either path represents a fraction of the original value.

Founder's Takeaway: Although I cannot find any evidence of a CVC ever blocking an otherwise successful sale of a startup through a carve-out, the possibility remains and is one to be cautious of. Founders should be careful when looking at carve-out provisions, and push back against terms that allow unilateral blocking of a sale with significant force. If the CVC insists on some form of protection, a founder should propose alternatives. For example, a more acceptable compromise might be a clause that allows the CVC to be dragged into the sale, but grants them a **Carve-Out from Non-Compete,** which is a much more common side letter term. This is far less likely to be a deal-killer than a right to refuse the sale entirely. If the CVC insists, ask for buy-out options and sunset windows to give you more options.

Deal Term: Change of Control Provisions—Change of Control of the CVC's Parent Company (Reverse Change of Control)

Mechanics: This less-discussed change of control provision addresses what happens if the CVC's parent company itself is acquired by or merges with another entity, particularly one that is a competitor to the startup. These remain rare, due to the inherent stability of large corporates that are capable of fielding a CVC arm, but a well-drafted clause can trigger a set of protective measures for the startup, such as the automatic termination of the CVC's information and board/observer rights, or an option for the startup to repurchase the CVC's shares at fair market value.

Startup Motivation: The startup's motivation is purely defensive. Throughout the relationship, the startup shares its most confidential product, customer, and strategic information with its CVC investor. If the CVC's parent is acquired, there is a significant risk that this sensitive data could inadvertently or intentionally end up in the hands of a new corporate parent that competes directly with the startup. This provision acts as a firewall, severing the information channels at the moment the conflict of interest arises.

Implications for the Startup: Without this protective language, a startup could find itself in the nightmarish scenario of having a direct competitor suddenly gain an investor's-eye view into its boardroom and data room. In technology, AI, and life sciences, where even limited data exposure can erode a competitive advantage, this risk can be substantial. However, it is rare for a startup to get these rights due to the natural power imbalance between a CVC and a startup.

Recommendations for Startups

- **Ask for a "Competitor Reverse Change of Control" Clause**: Ensure your legal documents specify that all information, board, and observer rights of the CVC terminate automatically if its parent becomes a competitor through a merger or acquisition.
- **Negotiate a Buyback Right**: For maximum protection, seek the *option* (not the obligation) to repurchase the CVC's shares at fair market value if such a change of control occurs.
- **Verify CVC Structure**: The risk is highest when the CVC is an embedded unit. If the CVC invests through a legally separate fund with strict, verifiable confidentiality firewalls, less restrictive terms may be appropriate.

Positive Scenario: The Firewall That Held

The Setup: CloudScale, a fast-growing B2B SaaS company, takes an investment from Enterprise Growth Partners (EGP), the CVC arm of a large, legacy software company, LegacySoft. CloudScale's savvy legal counsel insists on a change of control clause in the side letter that states if LegacySoft is acquired by a named competitor, all of EGP's board observer and information rights will immediately terminate.

The Interaction: A year later, the software industry is rocked by the news that LegacySoft is being acquired by a notoriously aggressive competitor, Titan Cloud: a company that directly competes with CloudScale. The deal closes, and EGP is now a subsidiary of Titan Cloud.

The Outcome

1 **The Clause Triggers**: The moment the acquisition is finalized, the change of control clause automatically activates. CloudScale's CEO sends a formal notice to the EGP board observer, informing him that, per their agreement, his observer rights are terminated, and he will no longer be invited to board meetings or receive confidential company information.
2 **Information is Secured**: While Titan Cloud now indirectly owns a piece of CloudScale, they are firewalled from its strategy. They have no access to board discussions, no insight into the product roadmap, and no visibility into the company's financials. CloudScale is able to continue operating without fear of its sensitive data being weaponized by its new, unwelcome indirect shareholder.
3 **Strategic Freedom is Maintained**: Because their confidential information is secure, CloudScale's board can continue to freely discuss strategies for competing with Titan Cloud. They have successfully neutralized the conflict of interest created by the acquisition, protecting the company's strategic independence and shareholder value. CloudScale can decide if they want to further isolate themselves from Titan Cloud by offering to buy back their shares or sell them on the secondary market.

Founder's Takeaway: You cannot control who might acquire your investors. A "reverse" change of control clause is a useful piece of insurance that protects you from a scenario where your trusted partner is suddenly absorbed by your biggest rival. It ensures that your boardroom remains a safe, confidential space to build your business, regardless of the M&A machinations happening in the wider market. Because this term is rare, a CVC may not readily agree to it, but it doesn't hurt to ask.

Deal Term: Early or Forced Redemption Rights

Mechanics: This is a right that allows an investor to demand that the company buy back their shares (i.e., redeem them), typically for the original purchase price or fair market value. The right is usually triggered after a certain period of time has passed (e.g., five to seven years) without a liquidity event, or upon the occurrence of a specific negative event, such as a material breach of the financing agreements, a failure to hit strategic milestones, or a key founder's departure. Redemption rights are a common term, usually requiring a board majority and excess funds to invoke, and it is extremely rare to ever see this clause activated. Early or forced redemption rights for a specific investor, however, are very rare.

CVC Motivation: The motivation for this term stems from the corporate parent's need for predictable liquidity and performance. Unlike institutional VC funds with ten-year life cycles, corporate balance sheets are often managed on a shorter-term basis. A CVC may be under pressure to avoid having "stale" or underperforming investments sitting on its books indefinitely. A redemption right provides a contractual off-ramp, creating a path to get their capital back if the startup is not progressing toward an exit or is otherwise failing to meet the CVC's strategic or financial expectations.

Implications for a Startup: This term is exceedingly rare in traditional venture capital for a good reason: it is incredibly dangerous. Startups are, by their nature, illiquid and cash-poor, reinvesting all available capital into growth. A forced redemption demand could trigger a severe liquidity crisis, forcing the company to drain its operational runway to pay back an investor. This can bankrupt an otherwise viable company. Redemption rights are common in most venture investments, but are rarely activated, and usually require a supermajority of preferred shareholders to agree. Any special redemption rights that allow the CVC to act unilaterally should be rejected outright.

Negative Scenario: The ConnectiFi Cash Crunch

The Setup: ConnectiFi, a hardware startup building a next-generation wireless chip, raises its Series A from a syndicate including Telco Ventures, the CVC arm of a major telecommunications company. Telco Ventures is excited about the strategic potential of the chip for its 5G network. As a condition of investment, they insist on a redemption right, exercisable after five years if no "liquidity event" (an IPO or acquisition) has occurred. The ConnectiFi founders, confident in their long-term vision, agree to the term believing it to be standard, but do not realize that the CVC can redeem its shares without a supermajority of preferred shareholders.

The Challenge: Hardware development is notoriously difficult. ConnectiFi makes significant technical progress but faces unforeseen delays in chip fabrication that push their commercialization timeline back by 18 months. They are burning through capital but are close to securing a major design win with a handset manufacturer, which would dramatically increase the company's value and set them up for a large Series B round.

The Conflict: The five-year anniversary of the investment arrives. ConnectiFi has not had a liquidity event. The management team at Telco Ventures has turned over, and the new leadership is under pressure from the corporate parent to "clean up the portfolio" and exit non-liquid positions. Despite ConnectiFi's promising technical progress, Telco Ventures formally exercises its redemption right, demanding its $10 million investment be returned.

The Fallout

1. **Sudden Liquidity Crisis**: ConnectiFi has only $8 million in the bank, intended to fund operations for the next nine months. The $10 million redemption demand instantly renders the company insolvent. All other investors' capital is now at risk of being wiped out to pay back the CVC.
2. **Fundraising Implosion**: The company's attempts to raise an emergency financing round fail. New investors refuse to put money in when they know it will immediately go out the door to pay off a redeeming shareholder. The redemption right has made fundraising for any new capital substantially more difficult.
3. **Legal Battles**: The other investors are furious, as the CVC's action is damaging their investment. This can lead to protracted and expensive legal battles between the investor syndicate and the company, further draining resources and management focus.
4. **Fire Sale or Bankruptcy**: Facing a catastrophic cash crunch, ConnectiFi is forced into a desperate fire sale of its intellectual property (IP) for pennies on the dollar. The company that was on the verge of a breakthrough is forced to liquidate, with the founders and other investors losing everything.

Founder's Takeaway: This is a rarely activated right, but granting a single investor the ability to unilaterally use it creates a massive, ticking liability on your balance sheet. Further, it distorts the CVC's incentives, especially as the CVC is no longer aligned with the other preferred shareholders. A venture investor's return should be generated by the company's ultimate success (through an M&A or IPO), not by forcing the company to liquidate its own operational runway to provide them with an early exit. Importantly, there are many other options to alleviate the concerns that this CVC may have. If the CVC must have some method of liquidity, offer them the option to sell their shares on the secondary market after a certain period of time, rather than redeem them.

Deal Term: Exclusivity Clauses

Mechanics: These provisions contractually restrict the startup's ability to engage in commercial activities (e.g., selling to, partnering with, or co-marketing with) with named competitors of the CVC parent. The scope can range from a narrow, time-bound restriction in a specific market to a broad, perpetual ban on working with a long list of companies.

CVC Motivation: The motivation is purely defensive and strategic: to block competitors from accessing the startup's technology and to create a captive commercial advantage or new capability that their rivals cannot possess. It is a tool to create a "moat" for the parent corporation, using the startup's technology as the barrier.

Implications for a Startup: Any clause that *broadly* limits your ability to sell to certain customers or enter entire product categories should be rejected outright. A startup's survival depends on its flexibility to pivot and pursue its largest market opportunities. However, a *narrowly defined* exclusivity can be a powerful strategic tool if it comes with a significant, guaranteed commercial commitment from the parent. Exclusivity clauses work best when narrowly defined by:

- **Scope**: What specific product or technology is covered?
- **Field of Use**: In what specific application is the parent getting exclusivity?
- **Territory**: Is the exclusivity limited to a specific geographic region?
- **Duration**: For how long does the exclusivity last? Is there a clear termination or exit ramp if the parent fails to meet its commitments?

Positive Scenario: The Focused Launch Partner

The Setup: A telecom infrastructure startup, "ConnectSphere," develops a new 5G signal optimization technology. They take an investment from the CVC of "SingaTel," the dominant telecommunications provider in Singapore. The side letter includes a two-year exclusivity clause for the Singaporean market, in exchange for a guaranteed $3 million licensing and deployment contract.

The Interaction: SingaTel becomes a true launch partner. Their regulatory team helps ConnectSphere navigate Singapore's complex telecom laws, their engineering team works hand-in-hand on the deployment, and their marketing department launches a major co-branded campaign announcing the "next-generation 5G network, powered by ConnectSphere."

The Outcome: The Singapore launch is a massive success. ConnectSphere gets immediate revenue, a marquee case study, and invaluable experience deploying their product at scale. During this exclusivity period, they can use their success in Singapore as a powerful calling card to sign deals with providers in Europe and North America. When the two-year exclusivity period ends, they can then work with other Singapore-based telecoms in addition to SingaTel. The limited exclusivity was a small price to pay for a committed, revenue-generating partner who de-risked their initial market entry.

Negative Scenario: The Golden Handcuffs

The Setup: HealthRecord, a startup creating a universal API for electronic health records (EHR), takes a seed investment from HospitalChain Ventures, the CVC of HospitalChain, a large, national hospital network. The side letter includes a clause granting HospitalChain exclusive use of the technology within the "healthcare provider market" for five years.

The Interaction: The founders, eager for their first big customer, agree. They spend the next 18 months deeply integrating their API with HospitalChain's proprietary EHR system. The deployment is a technical success.

The Fallout

1. **Market Lock-Out**: HealthRecord's sales team turns its attention to other hospital systems, only to be shut down. They cannot expand within the United States, their primary market, because of exclusivity with HospitalChain.
2. **Product Stagnation**: Locked into a single customer's ecosystem, HealthRecord's product roadmap becomes dictated by HospitalChain's internal needs. They are forced to build custom features for one client rather than developing a scalable, market-wide platform. Their efforts to grow organically in secondary markets like Europe are stifled by the dramatically different medical system regulations there.
3. **Venture Ambitions Die**: The broad exclusivity clause has locked them out of 90% of their addressable market. The startup, which had the potential to become the industry standard, has been reduced to a feature of a single customer, and in the five years that it has been hampered by this exclusivity agreement, new "copycat" competitors have formed and taken much of the market from HealthRecord, even though they have an inferior product.

Founder's Takeaway: Exclusivity can be a powerful tool or a vice that limits growth, and the difference lies entirely in the scope. Broad, market-defining exclusivity should be avoided, as it trades long-term potential for a short-term partnership. However, narrowly defined, time-bound exclusivity in a specific geography or vertical can be a smart trade, especially if it is paired with a significant, guaranteed commercial commitment that provides the revenue and validation needed to conquer the rest of the market later. It is best to avoid exclusivity in the largest markets, but the trade-off is generally worth it to have a launch partner in secondary markets, even if that comes with timed exclusivity.

Deal Term: Intellectual Property Ownership and Rights

Mechanics: When a Joint Development Agreement (JDA) or any form of technical collaboration is contemplated, the CVC side letter may attempt to pre-negotiate the ownership and licensing rights to the IP involved. These terms typically distinguish between **Background IP** (the technology and patents the startup brings to the partnership) and **Foreground IP** (the new technology and patents created during the collaboration). A CVC may push for outright ownership of, or a broad, perpetual, irrevocable, worldwide, royalty-free license to, any Foreground IP, and sometimes even to the startup's Background IP if it is improved or integrated during the project.

CVC Motivation: The CVC's motivation is to secure access to and control over technology that is strategically important to the parent's future. By obtaining broad IP rights, the parent corporation de-risks its own internal R&D efforts, gains a low-cost or no-cost license to cutting-edge technology, and can prevent that same technology from being used by its competitors. In essence, they are seeking to capture the primary strategic value of the collaboration for themselves as a direct, and often immediate, return on their investment.

Implications for a Startup: A startup's enterprise value is intrinsically, and often entirely, tied to the ownership of its IP. Granting overly broad ownership or licensing rights can damage a company's ability to partner with others, make it unattractive to future acquirers, and fundamentally undermine its business model. The ideal arrangement ensures the startup retains full ownership of its Background IP and all improvements made to it, as well as all Foreground IP developed, while the corporate partner receives a narrowly defined license for a specific, non-competitive "field of use," ideally in exchange for cash royalties. If pushed into a corner, a founder's safest fallback is to have the side letter merely reference that both parties will "negotiate in good faith" to come to "mutually agreeable" IP terms to be outlined in a separate, definitive JDA.

Positive Scenario: The Scoped and Royal-Bearing License

The Setup: BioSynth, a startup with a patented platform for creating novel enzymes, takes an investment from FoodScience Ventures, the CVC of a global food and beverage giant, GlobalBev. The side letter includes a commitment to negotiate a JDA in good faith. During the JDA negotiations, GlobalBev initially pushes for joint ownership of any new enzymes developed for their products.

The Negotiation: BioSynth's CEO, backed by experienced legal counsel, holds firm. They argue that their platform's value lies in their ability to be the sole owner of the IP they create. Instead of co-ownership, they propose a different structure: BioSynth will retain 100% ownership of the new enzyme's patent, but will grant GlobalBev a ten-year, exclusive license to use that specific enzyme *only* for applications in the carbonated beverage market, in exchange for a 3% royalty on the net sales of any product using the enzyme.

The Outcome: GlobalBev agrees. The structure is a win-win. BioSynth retains ownership of its core IP, allowing them to develop other enzymes for different applications (e.g., in pharmaceuticals or industrial processes) without conflict. They also secure a long-term, high-margin revenue stream from the royalties. GlobalBev, in turn, gets exclusive access to a breakthrough ingredient that gives their new product line a significant competitive advantage in their target market. The partnership is a commercial success, and BioSynth's clear IP ownership makes it an attractive acquisition target for a larger biotech firm a few years later.

Negative Scenario: The IP Giveaway

The Setup: QuantumSecure, a startup developing a new post-quantum encryption algorithm, is raising its seed round. They are struggling to find a lead investor but get a term sheet from FinTech Corp Ventures, the CVC of a major bank, MegaBank. The side letter, however, contains a seemingly innocuous clause granting MegaBank a "perpetual, irrevocable, worldwide, royalty-free, non-exclusive license to use any and all of the company's current and future technology for internal business purposes."

The Negotiation: The QuantumSecure founders, desperate for capital and validation, are swayed by the CVC's argument that this is "just for internal use" and is a "standard request for a strategic partner." They agree to the term.

The Fallout

1 **The Cornerstone Customer is Lost**: The investment closes. MegaBank becomes a user of QuantumSecure's technology, but they will never be a paying customer. They have a free, perpetual license.
2 **Market Value is Undermined**: When QuantumSecure goes to sell its product to other banks, the negotiations are incredibly difficult. Their competitors argue, "Why should we pay you millions of dollars a year

when your own investor, MegaBank, is using the exact same technology for free? Clearly, the market price is zero." The royalty-free license has anchored the perceived value of their product at nothing.

3 **Acquisition Prospects Evaporate**: Two years later, a large cybersecurity firm, CyberGuard, looks to acquire QuantumSecure. During due diligence, they discover the perpetual, royalty-free license held by MegaBank. The deal immediately sours. CyberGuard's M&A team realizes they cannot fully monetize the technology, as a major segment of the financial services market is effectively locked out. The acquisition is called off, and QuantumSecure's enterprise value is permanently impaired by a single clause in an early side letter.

Founder's Takeaway: Your IP is your company's crown jewel; do not give it away for free. A CVC investment is a purchase of equity, not a purchase of your technology. Any license to your IP should be treated as a distinct commercial transaction, negotiated at arm's length, and compensated at a fair market value. In any discussion of IP licensing, it is also important to set clear limits on the scope of use.

Deal Term: Operational and Strategic Information

Mechanics: This right goes beyond standard financials (which are typically covered in **Major Investor Rights**, covered in the previous chapter) to grant the CVC access to specific, non-public operational data or Key Performance Indicators (KPIs). The scope can be vast, ranging from relatively benign metrics like manufacturing yields to highly sensitive information like user engagement funnels, sales pipeline data, customer churn rates, or even detailed product roadmaps. This information is often shared directly with the CVC's parent corporation, a detail that is usually made explicit in the side letter's language.

CVC Motivation: The CVC's motivation is primarily strategic. While the data helps them monitor the operational health of their investment, its main purpose is to feed market intelligence back to the parent corporation. It allows the parent to keep a real-time pulse on emerging technologies, customer behaviors, and market trends without having to fund expensive internal research projects. In essence, the startup becomes a live-fire market experiment, and the parent gets a front-row seat to the results.

Implications for a Startup: Founders should always operate under the assumption that any information shared will be analyzed by the parent company's most senior strategists. The danger lies in providing a potential competitor with a real-time, low-cost market research department, effectively handing them the blueprint to your business model and go-to-market strategy. If you must agree to this term, the scope should be aggressively narrowed. For example, instead of providing "all operational KPIs," you might agree to provide "quarterly updates on top-line manufacturing yield and aggregate, anonymized user growth." Never agree to share customer lists, detailed pricing strategies, or your specific product roadmap with a CVC whose parent could potentially compete with you, because in all likelihood, if you are successful, they will.

Positive Scenario: The Technical Validation Loop

The Setup: "AmpereX," a startup developing a new battery chemistry for electric vehicles, takes a Series A investment from "AutoMobility Ventures," the CVC of a major automotive OEM. The side letter includes a right for the parent company to receive quarterly reports on specific, pre-defined technical KPIs: "cell energy density, charge/discharge cycle life, and thermal stability under load."

The Interaction: The data sharing becomes a powerful validation and feedback mechanism. AmpereX provides the data from their lab tests. The auto OEM's world-class battery engineering team reviews the results and provides invaluable feedback, suggesting that they have exceeded their minimum goals for cycle life, saying "your batteries last twice as long as the rest of the car," and that their primary focus now should shift to adjusting cell chemistry for greater energy density.

The Outcome: The collaboration accelerates AmpereX's commercialization. The shared technical data builds deep trust and allows the OEM to get comfortable with the technology's performance and reliability. Eighteen months later, the OEM signs a massive joint development and offtake agreement to co-develop a battery pack for their next-generation EV platform, securing AmpereX's future and making them a leader in the industry. The narrowly scoped, technical information sharing was a catalyst for a deep, mutually beneficial partnership.

Negative Scenario: The Free Market Research Department

The Setup: "QuickPlate," a startup creating a disruptive "ghost kitchen" platform for food delivery, takes a seed investment from "Slice Ventures," the CVC of global fast-food giant "SquareTable Pizza." The side letter grants SquareTable the right to receive "monthly reports on all key business and user metrics," including customer acquisition cost, user demographics, order frequency, and basket size by cuisine type.

The Interaction: The founders, excited by the partnership, diligently provide the detailed monthly reports. They see it as a way to show traction to their strategic investor and early customer. The data is a goldmine for SquareTable's corporate strategy team, especially information on the sale of pizzas.

The Fallout

1 **Strategic Blueprint Revealed**: SquareTable's strategy team analyzes the QuickPlate data and gains a perfect, low-cost picture of the emerging ghost kitchen market. They learn exactly which customer demographics are most profitable, which cuisines have the highest repeat order rates, how long customers will wait for delivery (and thus how large an area a ghost kitchen can service), and which marketing channels are most effective, all without spending a single dollar on their own market research.
2 **The "Fast Follower" Emerges**: Armed with this data, SquareTable bypasses the risky and expensive learning phase that QuickPlate went through. They launch their own, well-funded ghost kitchen brand, "PizzaDash," targeting the exact same profitable customer segments and cuisines that QuickPlate's data revealed were most successful. They even know where to build their ghost kitchens and how to make the best advertising campaigns to capture them.
3 **The Startup is Boxed Out**: PizzaDash, backed by SquareTable's massive marketing budget and brand recognition, quickly saturates the market. QuickPlate, the innovator, finds itself unable to compete with the incumbent it unwittingly educated. When QuickPlate goes to raise its Series A, new investors are spooked by the direct competition from a major food player, let alone the startup's own strategic partner. Investors worry that PizzaDash may expand to other cuisine types and push QuickPlate out of business, and so QuickPlate fails to secure funding.

Founder's Takeaway: Be paranoid about your data; it is one of your most valuable assets. While sharing high-level financials with investors is standard, sharing granular operational KPIs with a strategic CVC can be equivalent to giving away your company's playbook. Limit what you share to details that help build your partnership. Startups founded primarily around a business model innovation (rather than a product innovation) should be especially wary of sharing adoption data with the incumbents they seek to disrupt, particularly if they lack a strong technical moat. The danger lies in providing a potential competitor with a real-time, low-cost market research department. As a rule of thumb, it is okay to share information that you would include in a sales deck, but not information that you would want to hide from your competitors.

Deal Term: Purchase Obligations and Procurement Clauses

Mechanics: This term, embedded in a side letter, contractually requires the startup to purchase a specified amount of services or products from the CVC's parent company. The obligation is often framed as a multi-year commitment and can cover a wide range of offerings, such as cloud computing credits, software licenses, advertising inventory, or even raw materials.

CVC Motivation: The motivation for the CVC is multifaceted. Primarily, it creates a new, captive customer for the parent company, allowing the CVC to demonstrate immediate, quantifiable "synergy" and internal value. It also serves to effectively reduce the net cash outlay of the investment; if a CVC invests $2 million but requires the startup to spend $500,000 on the parent's services, the actual cash cost to the corporation is only $1.5 million. Finally, it deeply embeds the startup into the parent's ecosystem, making it more "sticky" and reliant on the corporate partner, increasing the likelihood that it will continue purchasing these services as the company scales. For this reason, many cloud computing companies offer free credits or sweetheart deals to startups with high growth potential.

Implications for a Startup: This is a term that should be viewed with skepticism. It creates a circular flow of capital where a startup is essentially using its own newly raised equity to buy services, potentially at a premium. This arrangement can lock a startup into using a suboptimal or overpriced product, preventing them from choosing the best-in-class provider for its needs. It can artificially inflate a startup's burn rate if growth is not as high as expected, and can distort key metrics, making it harder to assess its true operational efficiency. This term should be rejected unless the services are genuinely best-in-class, offered at a significant and verifiable discount to market rates, and the purchase requirement is minimal and well below the startup's own most pessimistic projections.

Negative Scenario: The FreshPaws Media Trap

The Setup: FreshPaws, a startup creating a subscription service for premium, all-natural pet food, is raising its seed round. They have seen impressive early traction with highly targeted digital marketing on social media and podcast platforms. They receive a term sheet from Global Media Ventures (GMV), the CVC arm of a massive media conglomerate that owns a portfolio of cable TV networks. The side letter includes a clause requiring FreshPaws to spend $1 million of the $3 million seed round on a television advertising campaign across GMV's parent company's networks within the first 18 months.

The Negotiation: The FreshPaws founders are excited by the prospect of a national TV campaign and the validation of the GMV brand. Their data-driven marketing lead expresses serious concerns, noting that their target demographic (urban millennials) has a low propensity for watching linear TV and that their customer acquisition cost (CAC) would be far lower (better) with digital channels. Feeling the pressure to close the round, the founders reluctantly agree.

The Fallout

1 **Massive Capital Inefficiency**: One-third of the seed round circles back to the CVC's parent company over the next 18 months. FreshPaws is left with only $2 million in actual working capital for hiring, product development, and other growth initiatives.
2 **Distorted and Damaging Metrics**: The TV ad campaign launches and, as the marketing lead predicted, performs poorly. The cost to acquire a customer via television is 5× higher than their digital channels, dramatically inflating their blended CAC. The company's overall unit economics, which were once healthy, now look unsustainable.
3 **Impeded Fundraising Narrative**: When FreshPaws goes to raise its Series A, the first thing new investors see is a high burn rate and a dangerously high CAC, a key metric that investors use to evaluate startups. The founders try to explain that the metrics were skewed by the obligatory TV spend, but the narrative is messy and sounds like an excuse. The VCs are left wondering if the team is incapable of efficient marketing, and they ultimately pass on the investment.
4 **Strategic Rigidity**: The company is locked into an ineffective marketing strategy. They cannot reallocate the capital from the failing TV campaign to the high-performing digital channels where they know their customers are. The purchase obligation has robbed them of the very agility that is a startup's greatest strength. The company eventually fails to raise its next round and is forced into a fire sale.

Founder's Takeaway: Purchase obligations indicate that the CVC may be more focused on propping up its parent's business units than on your success. The money you raise should be an agile and flexible resource for you to deploy in the most efficient way possible to grow your business. If you accept such a term, try to negotiate for a small purchase amount, a steep discount to what you could get on the open market, and performance-based opt-outs (e.g., "the obligation is void if the CAC from this channel exceeds a certain threshold"). Treat any such proposal not as a "strategic advantage," but as what it is: a reduction in your effective funding and a constraint on your operational freedom in order to secure funding and a beneficial partnership.

Deal Term: Retraction Rights (AKA Reputational Put Rights)

Mechanics: This is a very rare and non-standard variation of a forced redemption right. A retraction right, which functions as a form of "put right," gives the CVC the option, but not the obligation, to sell its shares back to the company for a nominal sum, such as $1. This right is typically triggered by specific negative events, which are defined in the side letter. These triggers could include the indictment of a key executive, a major regulatory sanction, or any event that the CVC, in its "reasonable discretion," believes could cause significant reputational harm to its parent corporation.

CVC Motivation: The purpose of this right is not financial but purely reputational. For a large, publicly traded corporation, brand value and public trust are paramount assets, often worth billions of dollars. If a startup they have publicly backed becomes embroiled in a major scandal, the parent company faces the risk of "brand contagion." The retraction right serves as an emergency eject button, allowing the CVC to quickly and publicly divest itself, severing all ties and issuing a press release to distance the parent brand from the controversy.

Implications for a Startup: While the direct financial impact on the company is negligible (buying back a multi-million dollar stake for $1 is technically a windfall) the signal it sends to the market is very negative. It is a public declaration of no-confidence from a major strategic investor at the worst possible time. The existence of such a clause should be viewed as a red flag during negotiations, as it indicates that the CVC's primary concern is not to support the company through challenging times, but to protect its own image at all costs. It suggests a partner who may abandon the ship at the first sign of trouble, rather than one who is committed to the long-term success of the venture.

Negative Scenario: The HealthGen Implosion

The Setup: HealthGen, a promising digital health startup, has developed an AI platform that analyzes patient data to predict disease outbreaks. They are raising their Series A and attracting interest from OmniCare Ventures, the CVC arm of a massive, publicly traded health insurance company. OmniCare sees immense strategic value in integrating HealthGen's technology. As part of the deal, OmniCare's lawyers insist on a side letter containing a retraction right, triggered by "any event causing material reputational harm." They frame it as a "standard brand protection clause" that is "never exercised." The HealthGen founders, eager to close the deal with their dream strategic partner, reluctantly agree.

The Crisis: A year later, an investigative journalist publishes a story revealing that in its early days, HealthGen used a dataset for training its AI that, while technically anonymized, could be reidentified to expose sensitive patient information. This problem had been resolved months before HealthGen launched its product. Despite the bug being patched and never harming patient data, the story goes viral, and the media narrative paints HealthGen as reckless with patient privacy.

The Fallout: OmniCare's corporate leadership panics. Their brand is built on trust and patient confidentiality. The association with a "data privacy scandal" is an existential threat to their public image. Within 48 hours, they instruct OmniCare Ventures to exercise the retraction right.

OmniCare issues a press release: *In light of recent revelations regarding HealthGen's data handling practices, OmniCare Ventures has exercised its contractual right and has divested all holdings in the company to protect the interests of our stakeholders and uphold our commitment to patient privacy.*

The effect is immediate:

1 **Market Collapse**: The public declaration of abandonment by its key strategic partner is extremely damaging to their reputation. Their abandonment signals to the market that the media story has credibility and there are valid concerns about HealthGen's privacy policies, even though they were fixed long ago, and before patients even used the platform. HealthGen's other investors, institutional VCs, are now in full crisis mode, unable to defend the company against such a public repudiation.
2 **Customer Exodus**: HealthGen's hospital clients, spooked by the news, immediately suspend their pilot programs, citing the now-validated concerns over data security. The company's sales pipeline evaporates overnight.
3 **Fundraising Halted**: HealthGen, which was preparing to raise its Series B, is now radioactive. No new investor is willing to even take a meeting.
4 **Talent Flight**: Key employees, seeing the writing on the wall, begin to leave.

The retraction right did not cause the initial data problem, but it turned a difficult, yet easily survivable, PR snafu into a near-unrecoverable blow. It allowed the CVC to not just leave the partnership, but to do so in a way that publicly condemned the startup to save itself.

Founder's Takeaway: A retraction right is one of the most founder-unfriendly terms you may encounter. It is a deal-breaker and should be rejected in almost all circumstances. A true partner provides support when your ship is taking on water; they don't hand you an anchor. If a CVC is concerned about brand risk, there are less destructive alternatives, such as the right to have their shares bought out or sold on the secondary market in the event of a scandal (at a fair price, with board approval, and without a public denouncement), but the unilateral power to publicly abandon a portfolio company for $1 is a sign of a fundamentally misaligned and potentially dangerous partner.

Deal Term: Veto Over Strategic Pivots or Business Plan Changes

Mechanics: A CVC may seek a side letter right that requires the startup to obtain the CVC's consent before making any "material" or "fundamental" change to its business plan or strategic direction. This is a "negative covenant," meaning it's a promise *not* to do something without approval. The definition of what constitutes a "material" change is a critical and often vaguely worded part of the clause, but it could be interpreted to include anything from launching a new product line to targeting a new customer segment or adopting a different business model (e.g., shifting from enterprise sales to a self-serve SaaS model). This is an exceptionally rare term and can be damaging to the long-term flexibility of a startup.

CVC Motivation: The CVC's motivation is rooted in self-preservation of its strategic thesis. The parent company approved the investment based on the startup's specific technology, market, and business model at the time of the deal. A pivot could render that original strategic rationale obsolete. Worse, the startup could pivot into a space that directly competes with one of the parent company's core businesses or another portfolio company, creating an unacceptable conflict. This veto right acts as a control mechanism to ensure the startup remains a strategic asset and does not become a strategic liability.

Implications for a Startup: This is a provision that strikes at the very heart of what makes a startup successful: its agility. The nature of early-stage ventures is one of constant iteration, learning, and adaptation. A startup must be nimble enough to pivot in response to market feedback, competitive pressures, or new technological opportunities. A CVC veto can lock the company into a strategy that is no longer viable, simply because it continues to serve the parent's original, and now outdated, strategic interest. This stifles innovation and can doom the company to failure. Even in situations where the parent company agrees to allow a change in strategic direction, its slow, bureaucratic approval processes can substantially slow the speed at which a company pivots and adapts, causing it to miss a critical market window.

Negative Scenario: The LogiFlow Dead End

The Setup: LogiFlow, a startup with a brilliant engineering team, has developed a sophisticated AI platform for optimizing the internal logistics of large, single-tenant warehouses. They attract a significant investment from MegaCorp Ventures, the CVC arm of a global retail giant with hundreds of massive distribution centers. MegaCorp's strategic goal is to use LogiFlow's technology to shave 5% off its internal supply chain costs. The side letter includes a veto right over any "material change in business model."

The Discovery: After a successful pilot in two of MegaCorp's warehouses, the LogiFlow team makes a critical discovery. While their tech works well for single-tenant, massive warehouses, their customer discovery calls reveal an exponentially larger market opportunity: serving the thousands of small and medium-sized e-commerce businesses that need a shared, multi-tenant warehousing and logistics solution. The data is clear: the future is not in optimizing MegaCorp's existing model but in building a flexible, networked logistics platform for the broader market: a "Shopify for warehouses." This is a classic, data-driven, and potentially company-defining pivot.

The Conflict: The LogiFlow team excitedly presents their pivot plan to the board, including their partners at MegaCorp Ventures. The reaction is ice-cold. A networked logistics platform for small businesses is not just outside MegaCorp's strategic interest; it's a potential *threat* to its vertically integrated supply chain dominance. The CVC, beholden to its parent's agenda, exercises its veto right, refusing to approve the pivot.

The Fallout

1. **Strategic Paralysis**: LogiFlow is now trapped. They are contractually obligated to continue serving a niche, single-customer market (large retailers), while their competitors rush to capture the massive, high-growth market they identified.
2. **Stalled Growth & Talent Drain**: Unable to pursue the larger opportunity, LogiFlow's growth flattens. The most ambitious members of the engineering and product teams, frustrated by the inability to build the product the market is demanding, leave for more dynamic competitors, or form their own new startup to address this more dynamic multi-tenant market.
3. **Fundraising Wall**: When LogiFlow attempts to raise its Series B, new institutional investors are immediately turned off. The side letter veto right is discovered during due diligence, and no sane investor will fund a company that does not control its own strategic destiny. The CVC's veto has made the company effectively "un-investable."
4. **Slow Decline**: Forced to serve a single strategic master, LogiFlow slowly transforms from a high-growth startup into a de facto outsourced R&D team for MegaCorp. The company either gets acquired by MegaCorp for a fraction of its potential value or withers away as the market it was forbidden to enter matures without it.

Founder's Takeaway: A veto right over strategic pivots is an existential threat to a startup. It cedes control of your company's most important function, the ability to adapt and find product-market fit, to an outside

Table 6.1 A table showing less common CVC terms and their relative impact on startups

Term	*Impact*	*Comments*
Carve-outs from drag-along provisions	High	Limit to a short, named competitor list if unavoidable; avoid broad opt-outs that can block exits
Change of control provisions—reverse CoC	Low	Ask for termination and data separation if the investor's parent is acquired by a competitor
Early or forced redemption rights	High	Mandatory or investor-triggered redemptions are non-standard and function like quasi-debt; avoid
Exclusivity clauses	Low–medium	Restrict narrowly in scope and time; broad exclusivity can deter partners and lower M&A valuations
IP ownership and rights	High	Keep equity docs free of IP grabs; in JDAs, define ownership and licenses precisely
Operational and strategic information	Low–high	Share things that help the partnership, don't share tricks to copy your business
Purchase obligations and procurement clauses	medium	Avoid hard purchase commitments if needed, convert to pilot milestones with opt-outs and clear service-level agreements
Retraction rights (reputational put rights)	High	Very rare; if accepted, cap timelines
Veto over strategic pivots	High	Limits your agility and ability to pivot, offer notice/consultation instead

party whose interests may diverge from yours. This term should be considered a non-starter and rejected in all but the most extraordinary circumstances. If a CVC is concerned about you pivoting into a competitive space, a much more reasonable alternative is to grant them a "Change of Control" provision that is triggered only if you are acquired by a named competitor, or to give them enhanced information rights so they have visibility into your plans. Giving them a proactive veto over your strategy is a recipe for disaster, and no reputable CVC will ask for this term.

Examples in Practice: The Win-Win Versus The Cautionary Tale

We have covered a wide variety of different terms, some beneficial, some harmful. To see how these terms play out together, it's helpful to see how they may work together in practice. The right combination of side letter terms can forge a powerful, mutually beneficial alliance, while the wrong ones can create a partnership fraught with peril. The following are fictional scenarios designed to illustrate these dynamics.

Positive Scenario: Drilling for Lithium

Consider "DirectLi," a deep tech startup founded by chemical engineers from MIT. They have developed a novel, patented direct lithium extraction (DLE) technology that can efficiently filter lithium from the wastewater (brine) produced by oil and gas operations. Their process promises to be cheaper, faster, and far more environmentally friendly than traditional evaporation ponds.

Their technology catches the eye of "Texas Petro Ventures" (TPV), the CVC arm of a large, regional oil and gas firm, "Texas Petro," which is facing pressure to diversify into clean energy. TPV's fund is a legally separate entity with a hybrid mandate heavily weighted toward financial returns.

The Blueprint for Partnership

TPV co-leads DirectLi's Series A round. The foundation of their partnership is codified in a comprehensive side letter, crafted not as a set of demands, but as the blueprint for a long-term strategic relationship with the following key terms:

- **Commitment to a JDA**: A clause committing both parties to "negotiate in good faith a separate, cash-paid Joint Development Agreement" to build a pilot DLE plant at a Texas Petro site.
- **Scoped Exclusivity**: In exchange for the JDA commitment, DirectLi grants Texas Petro a five-year exclusivity clause for DLE projects *only* within the state of Texas.
- **Narrowly Defined Information Rights**: A right for Texas Petro to receive quarterly updates on specific, pre-defined technical KPIs: "lithium extraction efficiency, purity levels, and operational cost per ton."
- **Board Observer Seat**: TPV is granted a board observer seat to facilitate communication and strategic alignment.
- **MFN on Commercial Terms**: A Most Favored Nation clause ensuring Texas Petro receives pricing on extracted lithium at least as favorable as any future customer.
- **Publicity and Announcement Rights**: A right for Texas Petro to approve any press release mentioning Texas Petro, the partnership, or the investment.

The Story Unfolds

The week after the financing closes, the TPV partner immediately makes good on the JDA commitment, facilitating a direct meeting between DirectLi's founders and the Executive VP of Operations at Texas Petro. Because the *intent* to partner is already established, the conversation is collaborative from the start. Within three months, they sign a multi-million-dollar, cash-paid JDA to build the nation's first commercial-scale DLE pilot plant at a Texas Petro site. This provides DirectLi with a huge infusion of non-dilutive capital.

Now, with a concrete, funded project to announce, the publicity rights are activated. DirectLi and Texas Petro issue a powerful joint press release announcing the construction of the pilot plant, framing it as a landmark step in creating a "new, sustainable source of lithium for the American EV supply chain." The news, amplified by Texas Petro's massive PR machine, lands in major energy and tech journals, positioning DirectLi as a serious player.

As construction begins, the board observer seat proves its value. When a permitting issue with a local water authority threatens to delay the project by six months, the TPV observer, who has deep relationships in the Texas regulatory landscape, makes a single phone call that clarifies the issue and gets the project back on track within a week.

A year later, the pilot plant comes online. The results are a resounding success, with lithium extraction efficiency 15% higher than projected. The validation is undeniable. The success, now public knowledge, attracts inbound interest from "Andean Energy," a major South American oil producer. Eager to secure the technology for their own diversification efforts and facing less competition in their home market, Andean Energy agrees to a long-term licensing deal at a price per ton for the extracted lithium that is 20% higher than the initial price set with Texas Petro.

This is where the MFN clause creates a win for everyone. DirectLi informs TPV of the new, higher market price set by the Andean deal. TVP shares this big strategic win with Texas Petro, showing that their early action secured Texas Petro a great deal. In turn, DirectLi had a price anchor with which to negotiate a better price with Andean.

When DirectLi goes to raise its Series B, their story is overwhelmingly compelling. They have a fully de-risked technology, validated at scale; a multi-million-dollar contract from an industry giant; and now, a lucrative international partnership that demonstrates global demand. The round is massively oversubscribed, and they secure a top-tier institutional investor at a valuation that far exceeds their initial projections. The side letter wasn't just a legal document; it was the strategic instrument that enabled their success.

Positive Scenario: A Doggie Data-Driven Deal

Consider "DogBite," a startup founded by a veterinarian and a data scientist. They've developed an AI-powered mobile application that allows pet owners to take a photo of their dog's skin condition. The AI analyzes the image, compares it against a vast database, and provides a preliminary assessment of potential issues, along with a recommendation to see a vet.

The technology catches the attention of "Best Friend Ventures," the CVC arm of "Global Pet Nutrition," a major pet food distributor looking to expand into the high-growth personalized pet wellness market.

The Blueprint for Partnership

Best Friend Ventures invests in DogBite's seed round. The side letter is carefully negotiated to align both parties for a future commercial collaboration and a potential exit, with the following key terms:

- **Commitment to a JDA**: A clause committing both parties to "negotiate in good faith a separate, cash-paid Joint Development Agreement" to co-develop an AI-driven, personalized nutritional plan feature.
- **MFN on Commercial Partnerships**: A Most Favored Nation clause ensuring Global Pet Nutrition receives commercial terms in the U.S. at least as favorable as any of its direct competitors.
- **Right of First Offer (ROFO) on Acquisition**: A right granting Global Pet Nutrition a 30-day exclusive window to make an acquisition offer *before* DogBite can engage in a formal sale process with any other party.
- **Carve-Out from Non-Compete**: A provision stating that in the event of an acquisition, Global Pet Nutrition will not be bound by any non-compete clause that would restrict its core business of selling pet food.
- **Data Protection on Change of Control**: A crucial clause stating that if DogBite is acquired by a named competitor of Global Pet Nutrition, the JDA will immediately terminate, and DogBite must return or destroy all proprietary nutritional data and formulas received from Global Pet Nutrition.

The Story Unfolds

Following the investment, the teams sign a cash-paid JDA. As part of the agreement, Global Pet Nutrition provides DogBite with unprecedented access to its most valuable asset: decades of proprietary research and specific nutritional formulas for addressing various canine health issues. DogBite uses this unique data to train its AI, evolving it from a simple diagnostic tool into a sophisticated recommendation engine. The new premium feature, "Personalized Nutrition Plans by Global Pet Nutrition," allows users to order custom food from Global Pet Nutrition directly in-app, and is a massive success.

The platform's success attracts the attention of "Wellness Co.," a large, publicly traded consumer health diagnostics conglomerate that wants to make a major entry into the pet market. They see DogBite as their perfect beachhead acquisition.

The ROFO is now triggered. DogBite's board formally approaches Global Pet Nutrition, giving them their 30-day exclusive window to make an offer. After a serious evaluation, Global Pet Nutrition's board declines to make a competing offer, preferring to remain a commercial partner.

With the ROFO period expired, DogBite is free to negotiate with Wellness Co. During due diligence, Wellness Co.'s lawyers review the CVC side letter. They pay close attention to the Data Protection on Change of Control clause. Because Wellness Co. is a human-focused health diagnostics company and not a direct competitor in the pet food manufacturing space, their legal team correctly concludes that the clause will **not** be triggered by their acquisition. They see it as a reasonable and narrowly tailored protection for a key strategic partner and not a threat to the deal's value.

Wellness Co. proceeds with the acquisition, purchasing DogBite for a phenomenal price. The deal is a huge success for the founders and all investors, including Best Friend Ventures. The side letter achieved its purpose: the JDA built a valuable company, and the carefully crafted change of control clause protected the CVC's parent from its biggest strategic risk without poisoning the well for a successful, non-competitive M&A process. Because Wellness Co. is not competing, neither party sees the need to terminate the partnership between DogBite (now Wellness Co) and Global Pet Nutrition.

Negative Scenario: Caught in a Steel Trap

Consider "AlloyForge," a startup founded by brilliant material scientists from Carnegie Mellon University. They've developed a revolutionary new steel alloy that is 30% lighter, 50% stronger, and, at scale, cheaper to produce than traditional high-strength steel. This technology isn't just an incremental improvement; it's a disruptive threat to the entire industry.

After struggling to get institutional VCs to understand their deep tech vision, they received a term sheet from "Global Steel Ventures" (GSV), the CVC arm of the massive, incumbent steel producer, "Global Steel Inc." The founders are elated to have a strategic partner who truly understands their market.

The Blueprint for Entrapment

The CVC, driven by a desire to control this disruptive technology, pushes for an aggressive side letter. The founders, eager to close their first round and feeling the pressure of their dwindling runway, reluctantly agree to a package of terms they don't fully appreciate the danger of:

- **An Equity-Funded JDA**: The side letter includes a detailed, multi-year scope of work for an unpaid JDA, effectively making the equity investment the sole payment for a massive R&D project.
- **Aggressive IP Rights**: The terms grant Global Steel joint ownership of all **Foreground IP** (new discoveries made during the JDA) and a broad, perpetual, royalty-free license to AlloyForge's core **Background IP** for use in "all steel-related applications."
- **Veto Over Strategic Pivots**: A clause giving GSV a veto right over any "material change to the company's primary business plan," which is defined as serving the steel industry.
- **Mandatory Management Access**: A requirement for "bi-weekly technical review meetings" with Global Steel's R&D and production teams.

The Story Unfolds

The investment closes, and the initial excitement quickly fades. The "partnership" begins. The JDA immediately consumes the startup; half of AlloyForge's small engineering team is pulled into daily calls and planning sessions with Global Steel's slow-moving, bureaucratic R&D department. The bi-weekly "technical reviews" become grueling interrogations, with the founders spending more time creating presentations for their investor than developing their product.

Six months in, a major aerospace manufacturer, "AeroSpace Dynamics," approaches AlloyForge. They are captivated by the new alloy's potential for creating lighter, stronger aircraft components. Aerospace is an attractive market with margins ten times higher than the commodity steel industry. They propose a lucrative, cash-paid pilot project.

This is the lifeline the founders have been dreaming of. However, when they present this opportunity to their board, the GSV representative immediately signals their intent to exercise their **veto over a strategic pivot**. From their perspective, AlloyForge's purpose is to make better steel for Global Steel, not to get distracted by the aerospace industry. The opportunity with AeroSpace Dynamics is dead on arrival.

The Fallout

1 **Strategic Entrapment**: AlloyForge is now trapped. The veto right has locked them into the low-margin steel industry. Worse, the aggressive

IP clause makes it impossible to partner with anyone else *within* that industry. Few competitors will pay for a technology that the market leader, Global Steel, can already use for free, and it is unclear if Global Steel will be willing to license it.

2 **The Un-investable Company**: With their seed funding depleted by the unpaid JDA, the founders desperately try to raise a Series A. However, every institutional VC they pitch passes immediately after reviewing the side letter. They see a company with no strategic freedom, whose core IP has been given away, and whose most logical commercial partners are already blocked. The company is deemed fundamentally "un-investable."

3 **No Competitive Acquirers**: With no path to new funding, their only option is to sell the company. But who would buy them? Aerospace companies cannot test out the product in advance because of the veto, making the acquisition much riskier. Other steel companies are not interested in acquiring a company whose key IP is already licensed royalty-free to their biggest competitor. There are no other logical buyers.

Trapped, out of cash, and with no other financing or acquisition options, AlloyForge is forced into a corner. Their only path for survival is to be acquired by their own investor, Global Steel. With no competitive tension and no other bidders, Global Steel dictates the terms, acquiring the company in a "fire sale" for a paltry price that barely returns the initial capital to the other seed investors. The side letter didn't just contain unfavorable terms; it was a perfectly constructed trap that ensured that Global Steel could neutralize a disruptive threat and acquire its groundbreaking technology for pennies on the dollar.

Negative Scenario: Makeup Can't Hide an Ugly Deal Term

Consider "Glimmer & Glow," a startup founded by two savvy brand marketers. They've created a new line of luxury, "clean-ingredient" cosmetics specifically for children and tweens, tapping into a burgeoning market that traditional players have overlooked. Their branding is impeccable, and their direct-to-consumer launch is a viral success on social media.

Their rapid growth attracts the attention of "Prestige Ventures," the CVC arm of "Prestige Beauty Group," a high-end adult cosmetics conglomerate. Prestige sees the "kid-luxe" market as a potential growth vector but is hesitant to invest the massive resources needed to build a new brand from scratch. Investing in Glimmer & Glow seems like a perfect, low-cost way to explore the market.

The Blueprint for Entrapment

The CVC pushes for a side letter with two key provisions. The founders, thrilled by the validation from a luxury icon and focused on the capital, agree.

- **Broad Operational and Strategic Information Rights**: The side letter demands "monthly reports on all customer KPIs, including detailed demographics (age, location), CAC by channel, lifetime value (LTV), top-performing products, and basket size."
- **Right of First Refusal (ROFR) on Acquisition**: A right for Prestige Beauty Group to match any acquisition offer from a third party.

The Story Unfolds

The investment closes, and Glimmer & Glow uses the capital to scale its marketing, rapidly expanding its customer base. As required, the founders diligently provide the detailed monthly KPI reports to Prestige Ventures. Inside Prestige Beauty Group, a dedicated corporate strategy team is tasked with analyzing this data. They are getting a real-time, PhD-level education in the kid-luxe market: who the customers are, how they buy, what they want, and how to reach them, all without spending a single dollar on their own market research.

Glimmer & Glow's success makes them a prime acquisition target. "Family Brands Inc.," a massive consumer packaged goods (CPG) conglomerate that dominates the family and baby care aisles, sees Glimmer & Glow as a perfect entry point into the premium beauty space. They begin confidential M&A discussions.

The Fallout

1 **The Auction is Chilled**: Early in the due diligence process, Glimmer & Glow's lawyers are obligated to disclose the ROFR held by Prestige Beauty Group. The M&A team at Family Brands Inc. immediately raises a red flag. Their VP of Corporate Development explains the chilling effect: "We are not going to spend the next three months and over a million dollars on legal and financial diligence to be Prestige's 'stalking horse.' We won't do their work for them only to have them snatch the deal at the last minute." Family Brands Inc. doesn't walk away, but they refuse to engage in a competitive bidding process, making a single, conservative "take-it-or-leave-it" offer that is significantly below what Glimmer & Glow might have achieved in a true auction.

2 **The Incumbent's Triple-Option**: Prestige Beauty Group now holds all the cards. The ROFR, combined with the deep operational data they've collected, gives them three ways to "win" at the startup's expense:

- **Option A: The Depressed Acquisition**. They can exercise their ROFR and acquire Glimmer & Glow at the artificially low price set by Family Brands Inc.
- **Option B: The Strategic Clone**. If they feel even the lowball offer is too high, they can decline to exercise their ROFR and let Family Brands acquire Glimmer & Glow. They can then use the year's worth of proprietary customer data they've collected to launch their own, well-funded competing line, "Prestige Petites," with a massive marketing budget, targeting the exact customer profiles they know are most profitable.
- **Option C: The Slow Kill**. If the market data shows the "kid-luxe" trend is a fad, they can simply do nothing, letting Family Brands acquire Glimmer & Glow, having spent very little to learn that the market isn't worth entering.

3 **Value Destroyed**: In this case, Prestige chooses Option B. They pass on the acquisition. Family Brands Inc. acquires Glimmer and Glow for a low price, but shortly thereafter finds a formidable new competitor in "Prestige Petites." The startup was able to exit, but at a relatively low valuation, further lowered as it struggles to hit earn-out goals due to a new well-funded competitor that already knows all their hard-learned lessons.

Founder's Takeaway: Be wary of any investor whose terms give them multiple ways to benefit from your work, even if your company fails. A CVC's investment should be a bet on your success, not a cheap option on your market. Broad information rights can turn you into an unpaid market research firm, and a ROFR can prevent you from ever realizing your company's true market value in an exit. Be especially cautious of sharing key operational KPIs when your key differentiation is your business model/ target audience, rather than a technology moat.

Strategy for Side Letters

A key principle in negotiating side letters is to create an asymmetry of obligation that favors the startup. Commitments from the startup should be framed with flexible, non-binding language, while commitments from the CVC should be as specific and concrete as possible. For the startup's obligations, phrases like "will use commercially reasonable efforts" or "will negotiate in good faith" are invaluable. They signal a genuine intent to collaborate without locking the startup into rigid, potentially burdensome actions. This provides the founder with the necessary operational latitude to navigate unforeseen challenges or pivot the business, ensuring that the CVC relationship remains a strategic asset rather than a contractual strait-jacket, especially if the corporate partner becomes unduly demanding.

Side letters are not an ancillary component of a CVC deal; they are often its very heart. They are the primary instrument through which strategic value and strategic risk are allocated between the startup and the corporate investor. As the examples above have shown, a well-negotiated side letter, crafted with foresight and precision, can be the foundation of a powerful, mutually beneficial alliance that accelerates a startup's growth trajectory in ways that capital alone cannot. Conversely, a poorly negotiated side letter, agreed to in haste or without a full understanding of its long-term implications, can become a ticking time bomb, encumbering the company with obligations that stifle its growth, limit its strategic options, and ultimately jeopardize its future. For the founder, mastery of the side letter is not just a legal skill; it is a core strategic competency.

Chapter 7

Chinese CVCs

For the ambitious founder, the sheer scale of the Chinese market can be an irresistible siren song. It represents rapid growth through an ocean of potential customers, fantastic manufacturing and scaling expertise, and a dynamic technology landscape with major players much more open to adopting bleeding-edge technology. This allure extends to its venture capital ecosystem, which has grown at a breathtaking pace. However, this chapter serves as a stern and unequivocal word of caution. While opportunities may exist, the risks for a non-Chinese startup taking on Chinese corporate venture capital are profound, asymmetric, and rooted in systemic differences that cannot be easily navigated or mitigated. At the time of this writing, for most Western startups, the answer to the question of whether to take on a Chinese CVC partner is simple: **Don't**.

This is not a conclusion reached lightly or based on isolated incidents. It is based on a pattern of behavior and a fundamental divergence in the principles that underpin the venture capital ecosystem. In mature Western VC hubs and especially Silicon Valley, the Venture Capital ecosystem functions because of a deeply ingrained, albeit unwritten, code of conduct built on reputational capital. Trust, while reinforced by legal documents, is paramount. This system works because venture capital is a "repeat game." Investors and founders live in a small, networked community. A VC who gains a reputation for being untrustworthy will see their deal flow evaporate, as founders will warn each other, and other VCs will refuse to co-invest with them.

In the still-maturing Chinese VC ecosystem, this foundational layer of trust and the importance of reputation are not yet as developed or universally respected. Simple conventions of trust that are common in Silicon Valley, such as taking a first VC meeting before requesting a Non-Disclosure Agreement (NDA), need to be abandoned when working with Chinese VCs. Whereas in Silicon Valley, VCs generally try to work hand-in-hand with their startups, using legal frameworks to clarify "handshake" win-win deals, the Chinese ecosystem often operates more as a cage match where legal documents are a hidden weapon or minefield for their startups.

DOI: 10.4324/9781003758280-8

The Specter of State Influence: The "Golden Share"

Before delving into specific risks, it is crucial to understand the unique political-economic context of China. The line between private enterprise and the state is intentionally blurry. One mechanism the Chinese government employs to exert control is the "golden share." This involves a government-affiliated entity taking a very small, often less than 1%, stake in a company. While seemingly insignificant, this share grants the government disproportionate rights, such as a board seat or veto power over key business decisions, particularly regarding data, content, and strategic direction.

For a startup, this means that any Chinese corporate partner, regardless of how "private" it may seem, can have mixed motives and divided loyalties. The strategic goals of the CVC's parent company may themselves be subordinate to the national strategic goals dictated by the Chinese Communist Party (CCP). This is a critical distinction. A Western CVC's "strategic goals" are commercial (e.g., build a better supply chain, sell more cloud credits). A Chinese CVC's strategic goals may be *national* (e.g., acquire key semiconductor technology to fulfill the "Made in China 2025" plan). In effect, every Chinese investor is a CVC for China, and every Chinese CVC may impose strategic goals for two masters. Whereas western CVCs have a fiduciary responsibility to their LPs to make money, and thus their incentives are at least relatively aligned with yours, Chinese CVC interests are aligned with the Chinese state, and may not be aligned with yours at all. This creates a level of uncertainty and potential interference that is simply not present in Western venture deals.

The Peril of Confidentiality and Intellectual Property

The Western startup-VC relationship is built on a foundation of implicit and explicit confidentiality. Founders share teaser decks with VCs expecting that this information will not be used against them, and later share their most sensitive data (financials, technological architecture, customer lists, strategic roadmaps) under the protection of NDAs and the implicit trust that a VC will not misuse this information. It is common practice for Western VCs to explicitly disclose any conflicts of interest they may have, such as investments in a competing startup, before a meeting, so that the pitching startup can tailor what information they feel comfortable sharing. This disclosure is a function of reputational capital; they do it to protect their own long-term credibility.

In China, this standard of confidentiality is not as deeply ingrained. There are countless credible accounts of information shared with a CVC being disseminated widely within the parent corporation and its network of partners and LPs. The very concept of an informational firewall is often disregarded, whereas in well-managed Western CVCs it is key to the structure of the fund.

This leads to the most feared risk for any technology startup: blatant intellectual property theft. The horror stories are numerous and consistent. I have heard the same story from multiple founders: a Western startup, deep in negotiations with a Chinese CVC, is asked for increasingly detailed product designs, source code access, or manufacturing processes as a final step in due diligence. The startup, eager to close the deal, complies. The term sheet is then abruptly pulled the day before the money is supposed to be wired. A few months later, a nearly identical clone of the startup's product, funded by the CVC's parent company, launches in the Chinese market. The startup has not only lost the investment but has also unwittingly provided the complete blueprint for its own competitor.

Furthermore, for a non-Chinese startup, the legal recourse in such a scenario is practically non-existent. Attempting to sue a large, state-connected corporation in its own domestic court system for intellectual property theft is a multi-year, multi-million-dollar battle you are almost certain to lose. The risk is not just that your intellectual property (IP) will be stolen, but that you will have no way to fight back.

The Fluidity of Agreements and "Landmine" Legals

In Silicon Valley, a signed term sheet, while not legally binding in most respects, is a powerful moral commitment. A VC firm that regularly pulls term sheets without just cause would see its reputation destroyed, and its deal flow would evaporate. In China, pulling a term sheet is often viewed as a normal part of business negotiation: a tactic rather than a breach of faith.

This transactional approach extends to the legal documents themselves. I have personally attended events where partners at Chinese law firms, speaking to an audience of VCs, have openly bragged about their skill in hiding "landmines" within legal agreements. Their pitches centered on how these hidden clauses could be triggered later to allow their VC clients to take control of a portfolio company, dilute founders, or seize assets if performance targets were not met. The lawyers were genuinely confused when the Silicon Valley investors in the audience reacted with horror rather than admiration. This anecdote reveals a fundamental philosophical divide: in Silicon Valley, the goal is to create a fair and aligned partnership, using legal documents to cement their mutually beneficial relationship, but in China the goal is to use legal documents as a weapon to ensure the investor can win at any cost.

Founder Diligence

Many Chinese funds are acutely aware of their tarnished reputation in the West. In response, a common tactic is to rebrand as an "American" or "global" fund. They may set up an office in Delaware or the Cayman Islands, hire Western-facing partners, and build a sleek English-language website.

However, this can be a thin veneer over the same problematic practices. Founders must be exceptionally cautious with any fund that has a limited track record or an opaque structure. It is essential to ask hard questions: Who are the Limited Partners (LPs) in this fund? Where does the capital actually originate? Is it private capital, or does it trace back to state-owned enterprises or government entities? A legitimate CVC fund will be transparent, and often proud, about its capital base. After all, their capital base represents a commitment from their parent company to innovate and work with startups. A CVC that is evasive about its LPs is a major red flag.

Beyond the risk of IP theft, founders of deep tech or "dual-use" technology companies (e.g., AI, robotics, semiconductors, aerospace) face another critical danger: CFIUS. The Committee on Foreign Investment in the United States (CFIUS) is a federal body that reviews foreign investments for national security concerns. Taking capital from a Chinese entity, even one branded as a "global" fund, can place your startup on the CFIUS radar. This can jeopardize your ability to receive U.S. government contracts, prevent you from being acquired by a U.S. defense or aerospace company, or, in the worst-case scenario, force the Chinese CVC to divest from your company at a later date, creating a massive legal and cap table crisis.

For a founder, navigating this landscape is a minefield. The allure of the Chinese market is powerful, but the potential cost of a misstep is catastrophic. Unless you have a team with deep, trusted experience in China and a compelling, market-specific reason to take on these risks, the prudent path is to seek capital from ecosystems where the rules of engagement, both written and unwritten, are built on a foundation of mutual respect and aligned incentives.

Chapter 8

Homework and Due Diligence

The preceding chapters have explored the complex landscape of corporate venture capital: the opportunities, the structures, and the potential pitfalls. This chapter is your operational playbook for preparing for and navigating the crucial first meetings with a corporate venture capital firm (CVC), transforming abstract knowledge into a tangible strategic advantage. Venture capital is fundamentally a two-way street; just as the investor performs exhaustive due diligence on every aspect of your startup, you must perform equally rigorous diligence on them. This is not a mere formality, but a critical exercise in partner selection that will have lasting consequences for your company.

The work you do before you ever enter a meeting room is often the primary determinant of the engagement's ultimate success or failure. A well-prepared founder does not merely increase their chances of securing a "yes" and closing a round of funding. More importantly, they dramatically increase their chances of finding the *right* partner: an investor whose motivations are aligned, whose structure is compatible, and whose strategic value is real and accessible. A thoroughly prepared approach allows you to forge a relationship built not just on capital, but on a foundation of mutual understanding and long-term strategic alignment. This chapter will provide the tools and frameworks necessary to conduct this essential diligence.

Doing Your Homework: Preparation Is Paramount

Before you initiate contact or respond to an inquiry, you must undertake a thorough research process. A generic pitch, disconnected from the CVC's strategic context, will usually fall flat. A thoughtful, tailored approach is a powerful signal; it demonstrates that you are a serious founder who understands and respects the strategic nature of the partnership you are proposing.

DOI: 10.4324/9781003758280-9

Understand Their Entire Business, Not Just the Brand

Many of the world's largest corporations are far more complex than their consumer-facing brands suggest. What you see as a consumer is often just the tip of a massive iceberg of B2B businesses, supply chains, technology platforms, and internal operations that are not widely publicized. Uncovering these hidden facets of a CVC's parent company is one of the most powerful things you can do, as it can reveal unexpected and highly valuable partnership opportunities that other founders might miss.

Consider these less-obvious examples:

- **Kawasaki**: Known globally for its high-performance motorcycles and jet skis. However, Kawasaki Heavy Industries is a vast industrial conglomerate that manufactures ships, high-speed trains, aerospace components for major plane manufacturers, industrial robots, and massive gas turbine engines. A startup in robotics, manufacturing automation, or energy infrastructure would find a deeply knowledgeable partner in these divisions, which are completely invisible to the average consumer.
- **3M**: Famous for consumer products like Post-it® Notes and Scotch® Tape. Yet, this is a tiny fraction of their business. 3M is a science and materials powerhouse with enormous divisions in healthcare (producing everything from surgical drapes to advanced drug delivery systems), electronics (making optical films for LCD screens), and transportation (creating reflective materials for road signs and vehicles). A med-tech or advanced materials startup could find a valuable partner with them, but wouldn't know that if they only focused on office supplies.
- **Michelin**: The name is synonymous with tires. But beyond selling tires to consumers, Michelin operates a massive B2B services division providing data-driven fleet management solutions to trucking companies. They also have a high-tech materials division that develops things like non-pneumatic tires for industrial vehicles and even specialized soles for performance footwear. Their famous Michelin Guide, while known to diners, is fundamentally a B2B play in the high-end hospitality industry.

Your task is to become a temporary expert on the parent company's entire corporate structure. This means going beyond their marketing website. Leveraging AI language models can provide a significant head start; prompting an LLM to explore and summarize the various business lines of a company, with a specific request for its lesser-known B2B operations, can rapidly accelerate this research. Ask it to dig into their annual reports (10-K filings), read transcripts from their recent investor day presentations, and analyze their M&A history to understand their strategic priorities.

This deep understanding will allow you to present partnership ideas that are insightful, relevant, and aligned with the parts of their business they care about most.

Define a Specific, Credible Vision for Collaboration

Armed with your research, you can move beyond a generic request for investment and formulate a specific, credible "Partnership Thesis." Your goal is to identify a clear vision for a partnership that is both compelling for your startup and logical for the corporate parent. The most effective way to do this is to look for precedents: Has the parent company engaged in distribution deals with other startups? Have they co-marketed complementary products? Have they integrated a startup's technology into their own platform? If you can model your proposal on a type of partnership they have already executed, you provide an easy, low-risk path for your internal champion to advocate for you.

While it is crucial to have a primary, well-reasoned partnership idea, it is also wise to develop a portfolio of potential collaboration concepts. Have a primary thesis, but also be prepared with secondary and tertiary ideas. This demonstrates not only deep thinking but also strategic flexibility. Your initial suggestion might be, "We see a powerful opportunity to integrate our technology into your logistics software, similar to the partnership you announced with startup X last year." This shows you've done your homework. However, be prepared to be flexible; during your first meeting, you will learn more about their internal priorities and capabilities. They may have reached out to you for a reason you haven't even considered, and your ability to adapt and explore new synergies will be a key indicator of your strength as a founder.

Prepare the "Hybrid Deck" for the Corporate Parent

A standard VC pitch deck is optimized to tell a story of massive, standalone financial return. A sales deck is optimized to explain what your product does and why a customer should buy it. When engaging a CVC, you need a hybrid of the two, a deck specifically crafted to speak to both of their mandates. Remember, the CVC investor often needs to generate interest and buy-in from the business units within the parent company before they can even bring a deal to their investment committee (IC). You can make their job dramatically easier (and faster) by creating a specific deck they can share internally, allowing you to control the narrative. This is not to say that you should not have a standard pitch deck ready when meeting with the CVC. If they are financially motivated, a standard pitch deck with added strategy slides is a great option. But you should also have a "hybrid" deck that they can share internally with other divisions of the company. The structure should be as follows:

- **Vision and Team**: Incorporate the long-term vision, targeted markets, and team slides from your **VC pitch deck**. This establishes that you are building a venture-scale business with the potential for significant financial returns, not just a feature or a consulting project.
- **Product and Value Proposition**: Pull the product-focused slides from your **sales deck**. Focus on the "what," not the "how." Clearly articulate the problem you solve, what your product does, and the value proposition for the customer (in this case, the CVC's parent). Use their industry's language and focus on the ROI you can deliver. For deep tech companies, performance metrics that would generally be too technical for a VC pitch may be important for their research teams to evaluate and compare versus their own efforts.
- **The Partnership Slide(s)**: Add one or two slides dedicated to the **potential partnership opportunities** you identified during your homework. You can include some specific ideas that you came up with, but this is a slide that you may revise after a first meeting with new ideas as you prepare information for them to share with their parent company. Alternatively, slides highlighting non-confidential partnerships made with other strategics can get the creative juices flowing and prompt the corporate to ask: "why aren't we doing this too?"

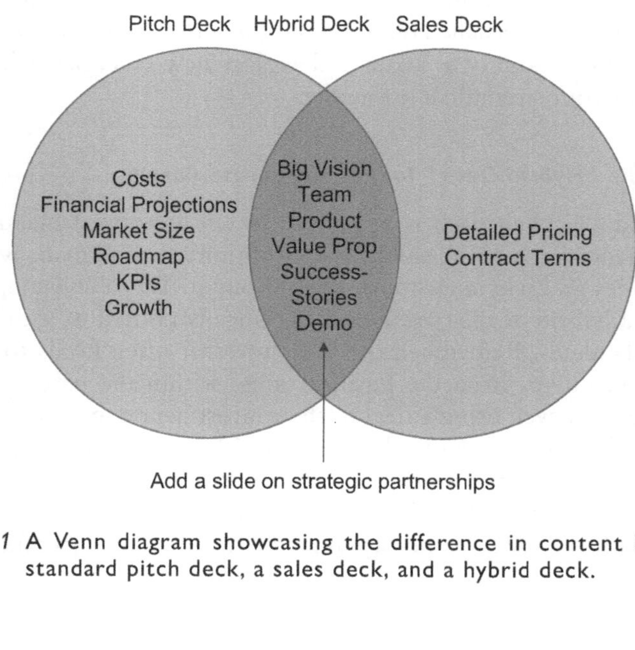

Exhibit 8.1 A Venn diagram showcasing the difference in content between a standard pitch deck, a sales deck, and a hybrid deck.

This hybrid deck equips your CVC contact to be an effective internal champion, armed with a narrative that speaks to both the strategic interests of the business units and the financial return requirements of the venture arm. Be prepared for this deck to be shared widely within the parent corporation. As such, it is wise to create a version that does not contain highly sensitive financial details. You may even want to explicitly call out which deck can be shared where (e.g., "Smallco pitch for BigTech Ventures.pdf" versus "Smallco pitch sharable for BigTech.pdf.)" If the CVC is incorporated within the parent company and requires a deeper look into your financials, that information can be provided later under an NDA in a secure data room.

The Founder's Due Diligence: Key Questions to Ask

The following questions are designed to help you peel back the layers and understand the true nature of the CVC you are engaging with. This is your due diligence. Listen not just to what they say, but how they say it. Transparency and clarity are positive signals; evasion and ambiguity are red flags. Use these questions to better evaluate the motivations of a CVC, how they operate, and most importantly, how they will act when in a partnership with you. Remember that this is not a comprehensive list, and you may want to add or remove questions based on the nature of your company and the nature of the CVC you are working with. View this as a starting point.

To Understand Their Activity and Cadence

- **How many deals has the fund done this year? How many companies are in your portfolio?**
  - **Why you're asking:** You're gauging their activity level and experience. A fund that does one to two deals a year operates very differently from one that does 10–15. A high volume suggests a well-oiled machine; a low volume may indicate a more bureaucratic process or a part-time focus.
  - **What to listen for:** A consistent, steady pace of investment is a good sign. Be wary of funds that have been inactive for a long time, as their capital may be frozen due to internal politics or their strategy may be in flux.
- **What is your typical check size and what stage do you typically invest in?**
  - **Why you're asking:** This is a fundamental question of fit. If they typically write $10 million checks into Series C companies and you are raising a $2 million seed round, the alignment is poor.

- **What to listen for:** A clear, defined range that aligns with your current fundraising needs. A vague answer may suggest a lack of a clear investment thesis. This could also be a signal to determine if you are too early to work with them and if their motivation is more focused on information discovery than investment.

- **Is this your first fund? How long has the CVC unit been in operation?**
  - **Why you're asking:** A first-time fund, even a CVC, is inherently riskier. They are still proving their model and may not have a clear process for follow-on funding or strategic support. CVCs, particularly new ones, risk being shut down if there are changes in upper management or poor parent company performance over a few quarters.
  - **What to listen for:** Experienced funds (Fund II, III, or later) and units that have been operating for 5+ years are generally safer bets. They have likely survived changes in corporate leadership and economic cycles. If it is a first-time fund, it is best to dig deeper into the team's personal track records and the parent's long-term commitment. Funds that invest off balance sheet are more susceptible to parent company performance. Funds that are GP/LP structure and independently managed are more stable.

- **Do you usually lead or follow? When was the last time you led a deal?**
  - **Why you're asking:** This sets clear expectations about their role in your syndicate. As noted previously, most CVCs prefer to follow.
  - **What to listen for:** Honesty. A CVC that claims to lead but hasn't done so in years is unlikely to lead your round. A clear "We prefer to co-invest alongside strong institutional leads" is a good, transparent answer that allows you to plan your fundraising strategy accordingly.

To Understand Their Process and Timeline

- **What is the approval process for an investment? Can you walk me through the specific committees and individuals who need to sign off?**
  - **Why you're asking:** You are mapping out the path to a "yes" and identifying potential roadblocks. Understanding the gauntlet your deal must run is critical.
  - **What to listen for:** A clear, well-defined process is a great sign. Be cautious if the answer is vague, like "it depends." Ask for specifics: "Is there a separate strategic review by the business unit? Does the corporate M&A team have a vote?" According to Silicon Valley Bank's "State of CVC" Report[1] only 19% of CVCs are able to make investments without approval from their parent company. There is likely a strategic process that this fund must follow. Identify it.

- **How long did your last deal take from the first meeting to money in the bank?**
  - **Why you're asking:** This is the most practical timeline question. It cuts through theoretical answers and gives you a real-world benchmark for your own planning.
  - **What to listen for:** An answer under three to four months is impressive for a CVC. An answer over six to nine months is a warning sign of a slow, cumbersome process that could jeopardize your financing round. Also listen for potential reasons why a deal was delayed, so you can understand what roadblocks you may face.

To Understand Their Incentives and Structure

- **Do you have external LPs, or is all your capital from the parent company?**
  - **Why you're asking:** External Limited Partners (LPs) often force a CVC to be more financially disciplined and operate more like a traditional VC, which can be a positive for founders. It is rare for CVCs to have external LPs, but when they do, it is a sign of great maturity for the fund and a history of good returns.
  - **What to listen for:** The presence of external LPs is a strong signal of a professionalized, financially motivated fund.
- **How is your team rewarded? Is it tied to the financial performance of the fund (like carry) or to strategic milestones for the parent company?**
  - **Why you're asking:** This question cuts to the heart of their motivation. It tells you whether they are truly incentivized to maximize your company's value or to achieve an internal corporate objective.
  - **What to listen for:** A compensation structure that includes a performance-based financial component (like carried interest or a phantom carry plan) is a strong positive signal. If their bonuses are tied solely to strategic metrics, they are likely to put a lot of effort into introductions, but their interests may diverge from yours over time.
- **What is the professional background of your investment team?**
  - **Why you're asking:** This is a critical proxy for the CVC's culture and motivations. A team staffed with professionals who came from institutional VC funds is far more likely to behave like a traditional, financially driven investor. A team staffed primarily with "lifers" from the parent company's M&A or business development departments may be more focused on strategic goals, less experienced in venture-scale governance, and more bureaucratic in their thinking.

- **What to listen for**: This is an easy question to ask, and usually part of introductions at the beginning of a meeting. Look for a blend, but ideally, you want the person leading your deal (the one who will take the board or observer seat) to have prior, professional venture investment experience. This signals that they understand market-standard terms, board-level conduct, and the founder's perspective. If the team is 100% internal corporate development, you should be prepared for a more strategic, and potentially more cumbersome, negotiation.

- **Does your parent company acquire companies from your portfolio? If so, how often?**
  - **Why you're asking**: This reveals their philosophy on partnerships versus acquisitions and whether they view the fund primarily as an M&A options pipeline.
  - **What to listen for**: A fund that has *never* had a portfolio company acquired by the parent might lack the internal pathways to make it happen. A fund where *every* successful company is acquired by the parent is a major red flag, as it suggests they may stifle other, more lucrative exit opportunities. A healthy, balanced history is ideal.
- **Do you reserve capital for follow-on investments in your existing portfolio companies?**
  - **Why you're asking**: This is a critical question about long-term support. A fund that doesn't reserve for follow-on rounds cannot support you through the life of your company.
  - **What to listen for**: An unequivocal "yes" is the only good answer, but according to a 2024 SVB survey,[2] half of all CVCs would answer "no." Not having reserves for follow-on investments shows a lack of sophistication and a CVC not taking their pro rata could be a negative signal to the market in your future fundraising rounds.

To Understand the Strategic Partnership

- **What are the biggest strategic priorities for your parent company right now?**
  - **Why you're asking**: This directly tests your strategic alignment. It helps you understand if you are a "must-have" solution for a top-level corporate initiative or a "nice-to-have" for a smaller division.
  - **What to listen for**: Specific, clear priorities that have been publicly communicated (e.g., in their latest earnings call or annual report). A good answer might be, "Our CEO just announced a major push into sustainable manufacturing, and your technology directly addresses that." Be wary of vague answers like "innovation" or

"growth," as they suggest a lack of clear strategic focus from the CVC's perspective.

- **Can you give me a few specific examples of successful strategic partnerships you've facilitated for your portfolio companies?**
  - **Why you're asking:** You are asking for proof, not promises. This forces them to move beyond vague statements about "adding value."
  - **What to listen for:** Specific, tangible examples with measurable outcomes: "We introduced Company X to our European sales team, which led to their first three international customers and $2M in new ARR," or "We gave Company Y access to our labs, which allowed them to cut their product validation time in half and secure FDA approval six months ahead of schedule." If the CVC cannot offer specific examples of how they tangibly helped a portfolio company through partnership, their partnerships may be much more one-sided helping the parent, or their motivations may be largely information-gathering focused.
- **How are strategic collaborations structured? Are they negotiated before, during, or after the investment?**
  - **Why you're asking:** This clarifies the linkage between the investment and a commercial agreement.
  - **What to listen for:** The best answer is that they are de-linked and negotiated separately. A CVC that includes a commercial deal in their investment negotiation can create bad incentives, especially if the investment is seen as a way to "pay" for the commercial deal. Ideally, the investment stands on its own merits, and the strategic partnership occurs if and when it makes sense for both parties. It is also useful to understand if, negotiated separately, the commercial deal is usually signed before or after the investment. That can give a peak into if you should prioritize commercial negotiations or fundraising negotiations first: Does a commercial deal greenlight investment, or does investment help push a commercial deal?
- **What are your standard side letter terms? Can you walk me through them?**
  - **Why you're asking:** This brings the most difficult negotiating points to the surface early, before you have invested significant time in the process.
  - **What to listen for:** Transparency. A CVC that is open and upfront about their standard requests (e.g., information rights, Right of First Refusal) is one you can likely work with. A CVC that is evasive or says "we'll figure it out later" is a red flag. The best answer is a CVC that looks for a very short, light side letter that states both parties will negotiate "in good faith" toward a future commercial contract, to be negotiated separately.

Notes

1 Silicon Valley Bank and Counterpart Ventures, State of CVC 2024 (2024), https://www.svb.com/globalassets/trendsandinsights/reports/the-state-of-corporate-venture-capital-2024-report.pdf
2 Silicon Valley Bank and Counterpart Ventures, State of CVC 2024 (2024), https://www.svb.com/globalassets/trendsandinsights/reports/the-state-of-corporate-venture-capital-2024-report.pdf

Chapter 9

After the Close

Congratulations! You have secured a syndicate of investors, navigated the complex diligence process, negotiated the term sheet, and signed a side letter that aligns your startup with a corporate giant. The money is in the bank. For most institutional VC investments, this marks the end of the hard part. The relationship now settles into a predictable cadence of board meetings and quarterly updates. With a corporate venture capital firm (CVC), the opposite is true. The deal closing is not the finish line; it is the starting gun.

The value of a CVC is not in their capital; it is in the "CVC Alpha," the strategic advantages that are supposed to help you build a bigger, more successful company. Those advantages are not unlocked by the signature on a side letter; they are earned through a continuous, proactive, and often difficult process of active relationship management.

A CVC is not a "set it and forget it" investor. If you are not regularly working with your CVC or its parent company, you probably should not have taken their money. CVCs are high-maintenance, high-potential strategic assets. The CVC partner you just brought onto your cap table has likely just fought a significant internal political battle to get your deal approved. They have put their personal reputation on the line, convincing their colleagues in various business units (BUs) that your startup is a smart bet. Their success, and yours, now depends on you helping them prove they were right. This chapter is your playbook for the "post-deal" world. It is how you move from a signed document to a genuine strategic partnership that can accelerate your business and help you win your market.

The First 90 Days: Seizing the Momentum

The period immediately following the close is critical. Your new CVC partner is your most enthusiastic advocate right now, and the internal "buzz" about your startup at the parent company is at its peak. You must use this momentum to build a foundation for the entire relationship.

DOI: 10.4324/9781003758280-10

The First 90-Day Playbook

- **Day 1: The "Welcome to the Team" Email**: The moment the wire hits, send a thank-you email. But do not just send it to your CVC partner. Send it to the CVC partner and the key "Internal Champion" or "Executive Sponsor" from the parent company's BU that sponsored and supported your company during diligence. This simple act achieves two critical goals:
    - It professionally links your investor (the CVC) to your commercial partner (the BU).
    - It frames the relationship as a three-way partnership from the very beginning.
- **Day 15–30: The Partnership Kick-Off**: Propose and schedule a formal "Partnership Kick-Off" meeting. This is *not* a board meeting. It is a working session with the CVC partner, their "platform" or "portfolio services" team (if they have one), and the relevant stakeholders from the parent's BU. Ideally, you have already been meeting with the business partners already as you scoped out strategic partnerships, but if not, the CVC can help as an advocate there, translating expectations back and fourth from the fast paced startup world to the more cautious corporate world.
    - **The Agenda**: The goal of this meeting is *not* to review your product roadmap. The goal is to agree on two or three tangible, achievable "quick wins" for the next six months.
    - **Examples of "Quick Wins":**
        - A joint blog post or press release announcing the investment and/or strategic collaboration goals.
        - A small, internal "tech talk" from your CTO to their engineering team.
        - An introduction to key team leaders that you will be collaborating with.
        - A clear, defined plan for a paid Proof-of-Concept (PoC).
- **Day 90: Deliver the First Win**: By the end of the first quarter, you must deliver on at least one of these "quick wins." Even a small, symbolic victory, like a co-authored white paper or a strong press release, is a powerful tool for your internal champion. It gives them something tangible to show their boss and proves that the CVC's investment is already delivering strategic value, and encourages the parent company to double down on building the partnership. Momentum is built on a foundation of small, early successes.

Managing Your Two-Headed Partner: The CVC Versus The BU

This is the most critical concept for a founder to master in the post-deal world. You did not just take on one partner; you took on two, and they have different motivations.

1. **The CVC Partner**: This is your investor. They sit on your cap table, may have an observer seat, and ideally are measured on both the financial success of their fund (either through IRR or phantom carry) and the strategic "wins" they generate.
2. **The Business Unit (BU)**: This is your customer (or channel partner). They are the operational counterpart within the parent company. They do not care about your valuation or your next funding round. They care about solving their own specific business problem, reliability, security, and not getting fired for championing a risky startup.

These two heads often want different things. The CVC investor (if they are financially motivated) wants you to grow as fast as possible to secure a high valuation. The BU customer may want you to build a highly custom, non-scalable feature just for them, or leverage your startup to build out as much business for themselves, regardless of how it affects your long-term value. Note that if your CVC investor is not primarily financially motivated, especially if they are a subdivision of the parent company's strategy department, their incentives may be more aligned with the BU customer than that of a financially motivated CVC. The differences between the motivations of the CVC and the BU customer are where the central tension of the CVC relationship lies. Your job is to learn how to use each "head" to manage the other.

A "Who to Call" Framework

Founders who fail to understand this duality often get frustrated, treating their CVC partner like a customer and their BU partner like an investor. Founders who succeed learn to navigate this, building a financial relationship with one and a commercial relationship with the other.

A Founder's Playbook for Land and Expand

One of the biggest potential self-goals is when a successful PoC fails to convert into a meaningful, commercial contract. The pilot is not successful enough to move into broader adoption, but is interesting enough where another business division wants to experiment as well. This can be especially

Exhibit 9.1 A chart listing which partner the startup should contact for a given problem or ask

Situation	*Who to Call*	*Why?*
You need to hire a specialized engineer	CVC and Institutional Investors	VCs are motivated to build your company, and some even include talent scouting and job listing among their value-add services
A Business Unit is asking for a custom feature that will break your roadmap	CVC Investor	The CVC understands the internal politics of the parent company and is motivated to help you grow. They can use political influence to realign the BU
Your pilot is a success, but you are stuck in procurement	CVC Investor	This is the reason you took the CVC's money. The CVC can go over the BU's head and apply pressure from the top down, while you apply pressure from the bottom up
You need technical data from the parent's R&D lab	Business Unit Champion	This is an operational request, all the CVC can do is direct you to the same champion
You are preparing for your next funding round	CVC and Institutional Investors	CVCs can commit their pro-rata early to signal their support and help make introductions to other investors
You need access to a special tool or resource	Business Unit Champion	CVCs do not have these resources; business units do. They are best able to help, especially as you build a working relationship
I need a reference call for a customer	Business Unit Champion	The Business Unit is your customer, and therefore is the best situated to give a reference for the quality of your work
I need a reference call for an investor	CVC Investor	Although the BU is your real customer, you do not want to overwhelm them with questions from investors that are not relevant to the product. Offer an introduction to your CVC instead, who can then pass them on to the BU champion if they really need that for diligence. Most times, they want to know more about the partnership, and the CVC is incentivized to make you look good

perilous in unpaid pilots, where the startup is spending resources to support a "customer" who isn't paying, all while its CVC investor looks on.

This happens because, for a BU manager, a pilot is a low-risk "innovation" win. A multi-million-dollar commercial contract, however, requires a real budget, a procurement battle, and puts their own reputation on the line. The default action is always to delay. Your job is to make a "yes" the path of least resistance.

The Land and Expand Plan

1. **Define Success (and the "After") *Before* You Begin**: Never start a pilot, even a simple one, on a handshake. Insist on a simple, one-page agreement that *defines the terms of success.*
   - **Bad Wording**: "We will pilot the software for 3 months."
   - **Good Wording**: "IF the software achieves [99.5% uptime] AND [a 10% reduction in processing time] over a 3-month test, THEN the corporation agrees to [enter negotiations for a paid, 50-site commercial rollout]." This links the pilot to the next step.
2. **Always Charge for the Pilot**: This is a critical, non-obvious rule. Even a nominal fee ($25,000) is infinitely better than a free pilot. Why? Because a *paid* pilot forces the BU to get a Purchase Order (PO) and a budget line item. It moves your project from a "hobby" to a real, accounted-for project, which makes it 100× easier to convert to a larger, paid contract. A free pilot is a favor; a paid pilot is a business transaction that clears the way for larger purchases down the road.
3. **Use Your CVC as the Escalation Engine**: If your pilot is a clear success (based on the metrics you defined in Step 1) and the BU is still dragging its feet on procurement, it's time to use your investor. Call your CVC partner and say, "We hit all the metrics. Your BU champion agrees it was a success. But we're stuck in legal. Can you please help escalate this to the executive sponsor?" The CVC can do what you can't: walk down the hall and get the right people in a room to un-stick the deal. All CVCs are motivated to help un-stick the gears: financially motivated ones want to see you build up a customer list, and strategically motivated ones want to show concrete examples of how their investments are working with the parent company.

How to Manage Your Board Observer (The "Win-Win" Scenario)

Chapter 5 detailed the *risks* of a CVC board observer (information leaks, chilling effect) and how to act *defensively* to avoid potential issues in the board. This section is the *offensive* playbook for turning that observer from a risk into an asset. An unmanaged observer can become a liability; a well-managed observer is a high-bandwidth conduit to your most strategic partner.

The "Managing Your Observer" Playbook

- **The Pre-Board Meeting Sync**: This is the single most effective tactic. **Always** call your CVC observer two to three days *before* the board meeting. Spend 30 minutes walking them through the board deck. Board meetings should never have any surprises for your board members, and it is standard practice to send board materials a few days in advance for board members to review so the meeting itself can be more productive and everyone is prepared. This can be doubly important for working with CVCs.

- **Why it works:**

  1 **It reduces unnecessary questions**: They will be prepared, understand the nuances, and can speak intelligently in the meeting. They can focus on how to help you in a "big picture" way, rather than spending time asking minutia that is important to the parent, but irrelevant to the rest of the board.
  2 **It avoids ambushes**: You can "pre-spin" any bad news, explain the context, and answer their hard questions in private. This prevents them from being blindsided and reacting defensively or negatively in the meeting, especially if there is news of collaborations with their competitors that you are sharing with a strategic-first fund.
  3 **It's your "Ask"**: This is your best time to say, "As you'll see on slide 10, we're having trouble with [X]. Given the parent's expertise, who should we talk to?" You are arming them with a task to help you *before* they even enter the room, and might even be able to give you some extra progress to report to the board. Instead of "We are struggling with [X], [Y] can you help us?," the conversation turns to "[Y] has arranged intros with [Z] to help solve the issue we have been experiencing with [X]." It completely changes the dynamic.

- **Handling Inappropriate Questions (The Script)**: There is a chance that a CVC observer (especially if they are inexperienced or from a strategic-first fund) might ask an inappropriate question in a board meeting, such as, "What pricing are you giving to our competitor, [Competitor X]?" Questions like this can cause unnecessary tension in a board meeting, especially as they present a conflict between the fiduciary responsibilities of the members of the board, and the lack of fiduciary responsibilities of a board observer. The best course of action is:

  - **Do not answer it.**
  - **Do not get defensive.**
  - **Use this script**: "That's a great question. It's a bit too granular for this board-level forum, but I'd be happy to set up a separate call with you and your commercial team next week to discuss our partnership strategy."
  - **Why it works**: It is polite, professional, and reasserts your control. It acknowledges their interest but moves the sensitive, non-fiduciary conversation to the correct venue (a commercial meeting), protecting the integrity of the board meeting. Further, it is a subtle reminder that they are not a fiduciary, that there may be a conflict of interest, and that you will be acting in the best interest of your company, not theirs.

Leveraging Your CVC for the Next Round

Your CVC partner can be either a massive help or a huge hindrance in your next funding round. Your management of them will determine which.

- **Get the Pro-Rata Commitment Early**: Before you go out to raise, sit down with your CVC partner. Get their commitment to participate and, ideally, to invest at least their pro-rata amount. Getting this commitment early is a powerful signal of "insider validation" that you can use to build momentum with new institutional leads. In many cases, CVCs may face pushback from doubling down on their investment, facing scrutiny based on the "marginal strategic value" an additional investment makes. In this case, ask for a small check, as a token of support to signal their continuing commitment to the partnership. Even a small check can be a powerful signal versus a lack of any follow on.
- **Secure the Testimonial (The Real Prize)**: A new institutional VC will perform diligence. They will, of course, call your CVC investor. While an especially thorough investor will likely ask to speak with a CVC's BU customer, the vast majority will content themselves with a business update from your CVC. Here is an opportunity to dictate the narrative your potential future investors hear. It is paramount that you provide your CVC early with a detailed, high-level overview of where your strategic engagements stand in an easy-to-read format. Updates on sales, revenue, profit, and whatever other vanity metrics you can think of will be critical to how your CVC will tell the story of your customer relationship.
  - The VC doing diligence will want to know how easy you are to work with and how open you are with sharing information (they don't want to invest in someone difficult to deal with). By sharing relevant information with your CVC before their diligence call, you make it easy for them to sing your praises.
  - The VC doing diligence will want to know what the status of the partnership is and its potential to generate revenue. It is much easier for the CVC to simply share your cherry picked and optimistic assessment of the partnership, rather than digging through corporate bureaucracy and arranging calls to get updates with the team on the corporate's side of the table.
  - Venture capital is a small world, and any VC worth their salt will find a way to contact your CVC investor, even if you are not the one making an intro. Make sure your CVC has the material needed to tell the story you want before your new potential investors go into diligence.

Concluding Remarks

The CVC as a Strategic Instrument

Our journey through the world of corporate venture capital began by confronting a persistent and misleadingly simple narrative: the idea of corporate venture capital firms (CVCs) as "dumb money." As we have seen throughout these chapters, the reality is infinitely more complex, nuanced, and strategically significant. Corporate venture capital is not a monolith to be universally embraced or dismissed. It is a vast and varied spectrum of opportunities, structures, and motivations, ranging from profoundly valuable strategic allies to potentially hazardous partners whose interests may diverge sharply from your own. The goal of this book has been to equip you, the founder, with the framework to navigate this spectrum: to distinguish the strategic ally from the risky proposition and to engage from a position of strength, clarity, and foresight.

We have deconstructed the CVC model, moving beyond the globally recognized brand name on the door to examine the fundamental structures that dictate behavior: the source of their capital, the nature of their internal incentives, and their legal and operational relationship with the parent corporation. We have seen how these seemingly arcane, back-office details have a direct and tangible impact on a startup, influencing everything from the speed and predictability of a deal to the long-term security of your most valuable asset: your intellectual property.

We have explored the unique and often challenging terms that populate CVC side letters: the rights of first refusal, the exclusivity clauses, the expansive information rights, and others that rarely appear in a traditional institutional term sheet. These clauses are the contractual embodiment of a CVC's dual mandate. Understanding them, negotiating them, and knowing when to walk away from them is the key to forging a partnership that accelerates your growth without mortgaging your future autonomy.

But this guide did not stop at the signature page. We have also established that the deal's close is not the finish line, but the starting gun. We have seen that the "CVC Alpha" is not a static benefit you receive, but a strategic return you must actively earn. This requires a deliberate, post-deal

DOI: 10.4324/9781003758280-11

playbook: a "First 90 Days" plan to build momentum, a strategy to manage your CVC investor and your Business Unit champion as two distinct partners, and a clear set of tactics to expand beyond the pilot and secure a long-term partner.

Ultimately, the decision to engage with a CVC is one of the most significant strategic choices a founder can make. It is a decision that must be made not in the heat of a fundraising process, but with a clear-eyed, dispassionate assessment of your own company's needs and a deep, well-researched understanding of the potential partner's agenda.

If there is one central takeaway from this guide, it is this: **A corporate venture capital investment is not just a funding event; it is the formal beginning of a deep, complex, and operationally entangled relationship.** Unlike an institutional VC, whose primary connection to your business is often through board meetings and financial reports, a CVC partner is frequently woven into the very fabric of your strategic and operational reality. They can be your most important supplier, your most demanding customer, a critical co-designer of your product, or your primary channel to the global market. This level of integration can be immensely powerful, but it also carries commensurate risk.

It is also a profoundly human relationship, existing within a complex political ecosystem. The CVC partner on your board is not a faceless logo; they are an individual with their own career, their own key performance indicators, and their own boss to impress. Their dual mandate is not just structural; it is personal. A founder who understands this can turn their CVC partner into a true champion. By proactively providing your partner with the "quick wins," the successful pilot data, and the positive strategic updates they can report back to their parent and other future investors, you are not just managing them, you are arming them. You are making them look smart. You are helping them win their own internal battles, and in doing so, transforming them from a passive investor into your most powerful internal advocate to leverage their parent company.

Therefore, the onus is on you, the founder, to be the architect of this relationship. This requires more than a great pitch deck and a compelling vision. It requires diligent, exhaustive homework to understand the hidden corners and unspoken priorities of the corporate parent. It requires the courage to ask tough, probing questions about incentives, processes, and potential conflicts of interest. And, most importantly, it requires the discipline to walk away from a deal that offers a tempting valuation but comes with misaligned interests or dangerous strategic constraints that could cripple your company's long-term potential.

The most successful founders who partner with CVCs view them not as a source of easy money, but as a powerful, specialized instrument in their strategic toolkit. Like any powerful tool, it can create tremendous value when wielded with skill, precision, and a clear understanding of its purpose. It can open doors to customers that would otherwise take years to penetrate, grant access to unparalleled technical resources, and bestow a level of market credibility that money alone cannot buy. But wielded carelessly, without proper diligence, or for the wrong task, it can lead to strategic dead ends, compromised intellectual property, and a loss of the very independence and agility that make a startup special.

This tool must also be re-evaluated over time. The CVC that was the perfect, validating partner for your Series A may have terms (like a ROFR on acquisition) that make them a strategic liability when you are trying to run a competitive M&A process five years later. The relationship is not static. It is a longitudinal, strategic engagement that you must constantly manage, reassess, and align with your company's evolving goals. This is because your company's primary objective changes. At the Seed or Series A stage, your goal is often survival and market validation, and a CVC's brand and partnership can be invaluable. At the pre-IPO or M&A stage, your goal is maximizing enterprise value, which requires a clean cap table and zero conflicts of interest. The very terms that provided validation early on, like a broad intellectual property (IP) license to your anchor partner or an acquisition Right of First Refusal, can become the single biggest obstacle to a competitive exit. The terms you sign today will echo for the entire life of your company.

This concept can be thought of as "strategic debt." In the same way engineers take on "tech debt" to ship a product faster, founders often take on "strategic debt" in the form of onerous side letter terms to close a critical, early funding round. This debt does not simply disappear; it accrues interest. It may sit dormant for years, only to come due at the worst possible moment: in the middle of a high-stakes M&A negotiation. Your job as a founder and CEO is not only to be a visionary and an operator, but also a long-term capital strategist, constantly assessing and, if possible, "refinancing" this debt. This may involve using the leverage of a new, oversubscribed funding round to renegotiate old side letter terms, or even offering to buy back a problematic investor's shares to clean up the cap table before a final sale. The partnership, and the terms that define it, must evolve just as your company does.

Your goal is not simply to raise capital; it is to build a great, enduring company. The right CVC, chosen for the right reasons and at the right time, can be a powerful accelerant on that journey. By moving beyond the "dumb money" myth and embracing the complexity of the CVC landscape, you are no longer just a founder seeking investment. You are a strategist, making a deliberate choice to leverage the scale, resources, and expertise of the world's largest companies to achieve your own ambitious vision. Choose wisely.

Glossary of Terms

Accelerator A program designed to help early-stage companies grow rapidly over a fixed, intensive period, typically in exchange for equity. Accelerators provide mentorship, resources, and networking opportunities, culminating in a "Demo Day" for investors.

Accredited Investor An individual or entity that meets specific income or net worth criteria required by securities regulators (like the SEC in the United States). Founders can only legally raise capital from accredited investors in most private financing rounds.

Acquisition A transaction where one company purchases a majority or all of another company's shares or assets. This is the most common form of "exit" or "liquidity event" for a venture-backed startup.

Advisor An experienced professional, often a former founder or industry expert, who provides guidance and connections to a startup in exchange for a small amount of equity (stock options). Unlike a board member, an advisor has no formal power, but a good one can be invaluable.

Allocation The portion of a startup's financing round that an investor is permitted to invest. In competitive or oversubscribed rounds, securing a desired allocation can be a key goal for a VC firm.

Analyst (Title) A junior-level investment professional at a VC firm, often a recent graduate, whose primary job is to support the partners by screening new deals, conducting market research, and building financial models. They are rarely decision-makers but are often the first point of contact.

Angel Investor A high-net-worth individual who provides capital for a business startup, usually in exchange for equity or convertible debt. Angel investors are often the first source of outside capital for a new startup.

Anti-Dilution Provision A clause that protects an investor from their ownership stake being significantly diluted by future financing rounds at a lower valuation than what they invested at. These provisions adjust the conversion price of preferred stock to account for the "down round."

As-Converted Basis A calculation of a company's equity that assumes all preferred stock has been converted into common stock. This is used to determine the total ownership percentage each investor has in a company, especially in an exit scenario.

Associate (Title) A junior investment professional at a VC firm, typically with a few years of experience, who is responsible for sourcing new deals, supporting due diligence, and monitoring portfolio companies. They are more senior than an analyst but generally do not lead the deal process.

Background IP The intellectual property (patents, trade secrets, copyrights, etc.) that a startup has developed *prior* to entering into a partnership or joint development agreement. It is crucial to clearly define and protect this pre-existing IP in any collaboration.

Balance Sheet Investing A common CVC model where investments are made directly from the parent corporation's main financial accounts (its balance sheet), rather than from a dedicated, separate fund. This structure can tie the CVC's investment capacity to the parent company's financial performance.

Basis of Stock Option (See Strike Price). The price at which a stock option can be bought or sold (usually lower than the future anticipated price).

Board of Directors (Board) A group of individuals elected to represent shareholders and oversee the management of a company. The board has a fiduciary duty to act in the best interests of the corporation.

Board Observer Rights The right for an investor to designate an individual to attend a company's board meetings and receive board materials. The observer can participate in discussions but does not have a vote and does not owe fiduciary duties to the company.

Borrowed Conviction When an investor leverages the diligence and conviction of others who are more expert in a specific field to "fill in the gaps" of their own diligence process.

Bridge Round (or Bridge Financing) A small round of financing intended to provide a company with enough capital to "bridge" the gap to a larger, future funding round. It is often structured using a convertible note or SAFE to avoid the complexity of a priced round.

Business Unit (BU) A specific operational division or department within the CVC's parent company (e.g., the "Cloud Services" division or the "Automotive Engineering" team). Gaining "buy-in" and an "internal champion" from a relevant BU is often a critical prerequisite for getting a CVC investment approved.

Cap (Valuation Cap) The maximum valuation at which a convertible note or SAFE will convert into equity in a future priced round. A "cap" protects early investors from being diluted if the company raises its next round at a very high valuation.

Cap Table (Capitalization Table) A detailed spreadsheet that shows the equity capitalization for a company. It lists all the company's securities (common stock, preferred stock, options, warrants) and who owns them, creating a full picture of ownership.

Capital Call How a VC asks its investors (LPs) to send cash to make an investment or pay fees. VCs do not hold their full fund in cash but instead make capital calls as needed to invest in startups as they find them.

Carried Interest (Carry) A share of the profits of a venture capital fund (typically 20%) that is paid to the General Partners as their primary performance incentive. It aligns the interests of the fund managers (GPs) with their investors (LPs) by rewarding successful outcomes.

Cash-on-Cash Return A performance metric that measures the total cash an investor receives back divided by the total cash they invested. It provides a straightforward, non-time-weighted view of how much money was returned from an investment.

Carve-Out A provision in a legal agreement that creates an exception, exempting a party from certain obligations that apply to others. CVCs often seek carve-outs from non-compete clauses in M&A agreements.

Change of Control Provisions Terms in an agreement that are triggered when a company is acquired, or its ownership otherwise changes significantly. These can include veto rights or automatic share buyouts.

Clawback A contractual provision that allows a VC fund's Limited Partners (LPs) to "claw back" (or reclaim) money from the General Partners (GPs). This is used if the GPs have been paid carried interest on early, successful exits, but the fund's later performance is poor, resulting in the GPs having been overpaid their 20% share.

Clean Term Sheet A term sheet that adheres closely to NVCA standard, founder-friendly terms without containing unusual, complex, or onerous provisions. It simplifies negotiations and reduces the potential for future conflicts or complications.

Cohort A group of startups that participate in an accelerator or incubator program at the same time. This structure is designed to foster peer support and collaborative learning.

Common Stock A type of stock that has the least amount of rights, typically held by founders and employees. This is as opposed to preferred stock owned by investors, which has superior rights (like a liquidation preference). Common stock is valued much lower than preferred stock, granting major tax advantages to founders and employees.

Convertible Note/Convertible Debt A form of short-term debt that converts into equity, typically in conjunction with a future financing round. It allows a startup to raise capital without immediately setting a valuation.

Corporate Development (Corp Dev) The team inside a corporation responsible for executing mergers, acquisitions (M&A), and large-scale strategic partnerships. This team is often distinct from the CVC, but the CVC often works closely with them, sometimes acting as a "feeder" or "M&A pipeline" for their activities.

Corporate Venture Capital (CVC) A specialized form of venture capital where a large corporation invests its own capital directly in external startup companies. CVCs typically have both financial and strategic objectives.

Customer Advisory Board (CAB) A select group of key (and often early) customers that a startup invites to meet on a regular basis to provide direct feedback on its product roadmap and business strategy. These are powerful tools that enable rapid product iteration and pivots, while simultaneously building advocates among their customers. A CAB can be a powerful tool to offer a CVC parent deep strategic access and influence, serving as a meaningful alternative to a formal board or observer seat.

CVC Alpha The concept that startups backed by CVCs may achieve superior performance (alpha) due to the strategic value provided by the corporate partner. This value can manifest as increased survival rates, higher exit valuations, or faster growth.

Data Room A secure online location where a startup stores confidential documents (financials, contracts, IP filings, etc.) for investors to review during the due diligence process.

Deal Flow The rate at which a VC firm receives business plans and investment proposals. A strong deal flow is a key indicator of a firm's network and reputation.

Demo Day A culminating event for an accelerator program where graduating startups pitch their businesses to a large audience of investors and potential partners.

Dilution The reduction in the ownership percentage of existing shareholders caused by the issuance of new shares in a financing round.

Director (Title) "Director" is a common job title within a venture capital firm, often signifying a senior professional. In a CVC, this title often aligns with the parent's corporate hierarchy, making them likely a key decision-maker in investments. It is roughly equivalent to a GP in an institutional fund and may or may not include carried interest.

Director (Board) A director is an individual who serves on a company's Board of Directors, typically elected by shareholders (such as a VC fund) to represent their interests and provide governance and oversight to the management team. Unlike a Board Observer, a Director has a formal vote on board matters and is legally bound by a fiduciary duty to act in the best interests of the entire company and all its shareholders.

Distribution to Paid in Capital (DPI) A key performance metric for a venture fund that measures the cumulative cash returned to its Limited Partners relative to the total capital they have contributed. A DPI of 1.0× means the LPs have received all their initial capital back.

Down Round A financing round at a lower valuation than the previous round. This is problematic to the company's reputation and morale and can cause massive dilution of founders and previous investors without anti-dilution protections.

Drag-Along Provisions A provision in a voting agreement that allows a majority of investors to force all other shareholders to agree to a sale of the company. It prevents minority shareholders from blocking a desirable M&A transaction.

Dry Powder The amount of committed, unspent capital that a VC fund has available to make new investments or follow-on investments in its existing portfolio. A high amount of "dry powder" in the market can signal a competitive environment for deals.

Dual Mandate The core challenge of CVCs, who are simultaneously judged on two distinct goals: achieving high financial returns (like a traditional VC) and delivering strategic value to their corporate parent. This inherent tension defines their behavior and can lead to complex negotiations.

Dumb Money A pejorative term used in venture capital to describe investors who are perceived to lack financial discipline, overpay for deals, or add little value beyond their capital. It is often associated with inexperienced or purely strategic investors.

Due Diligence The comprehensive process of research, investigation, and verification that a VC firm conducts on a startup before making an investment. It covers the team, market, technology, financials, and legal structure.

Earn-Out A financial provision in an M&A agreement where a portion of the total purchase price is paid to the startup's shareholders only *after* the acquisition has closed. This contingent payment is released only if the company achieves specific, pre-defined performance milestones.

Economics A shorthand term for the collection of deal terms that directly impact the financial returns for an investor. This includes not just the valuation but also the liquidation preference, anti-dilution rights, and pro-rata rights.

Employee Pool (See Option Pool). A percentage of the company's stock (e.g., 10–20%) is reserved for issuing stock options to future employees, advisors, and consultants. This pool is a critical part of a term sheet negotiation, as its size directly impacts the dilution of all existing shareholders.

Entrepreneurs in Residence (EIRs) A program where a corporation hires experienced entrepreneurs to work on developing new business ideas internally. It is a tool for corporate innovation and talent retention.

Enterprise Value A measure of a company's total value, often used as a more comprehensive alternative to market capitalization. It is calculated as market capitalization plus debt and preferred shares, minus total cash.

Equity Equity represents a stake of ownership in a company, typically in the form of shares of stock (like common or preferred stock). In a venture deal, founders sell equity in their company to investors in exchange for capital.

Escrow A legal arrangement where a third party temporarily holds a portion of the purchase price in an M&A transaction. This fund is used to cover any potential breaches of warranties or representations discovered after the deal closes, protecting the acquirer.

Evergreen Fund A CVC model where the investment fund is continuously replenished by the parent corporation, often on an annual basis. This structure provides a steady source of capital, independent of traditional fundraising cycles.

Exclusivity Clauses Provisions in an agreement that restrict a startup's ability to work with named competitors of the CVC's parent company. These must be carefully scoped to avoid limiting a startup's market potential.

Executive Summary A brief, one-to-two-page document, not protected by NDA, that provides a high-level overview of a startup's business plan, team, market, and financials. It is often used as the initial "teaser" to get a potential investor interested in learning more. CVCs may ask for this to circulate within their parent company to identify interested divisions and generate strategic alignment.

Exercise The act of an employee or advisor purchasing their vested stock options by paying the pre-determined "strike price" per share. This converts the "option to buy" into actual ownership of company stock.

Exit (See Liquidity Event). The method by which an investor and/or founder realizes a return on their investment. The most common exits are an acquisition (M&A) or an Initial Public Offering (IPO).

Extension A small financing round that "extends" a previous funding round, often allowing a new investor to join on similar terms. It is a mechanism to add capital without the complexity of a full new round.

Fair Market Value (FMV) The price at which an asset (like a company's common stock) would change hands between a willing buyer and a willing seller, both having reasonable knowledge of relevant facts. This value is often formally determined by a 409A valuation to set the strike price for employee stock options. Preferred stock generally has a higher FMV than common stock.

Fiduciary Duty A legal and ethical obligation for one party to act in the best financial interests of another. Board members have a fiduciary duty to the company and all its shareholders.

Field of Use (FOU) A critical legal term in IP and technology licensing agreements that narrowly defines the specific market, product, or geography in which a partner is allowed to use a startup's technology. It is a key tool for founders to grant strategic access to a CVC's parent without giving away their entire market.

Financing Round An event in which a startup raises a distinct amount of capital from investors. Rounds are typically named sequentially (e.g., Seed, Series A, and Series B).

Flat Round A round of financing where the company's pre-money valuation is the same as the post-money valuation of its previous round. While not as positive as an "up round," it is preferable to a "down round" and signals that the company has maintained its value. These are often used in extensions or bridges if the company has failed to hit their anticipated milestones.

Forced Purchases A side letter term that contractually requires a startup to purchase a certain amount of services from the CVC's parent company. This can create a conflict of interest and should be approached with caution.

Foreground IP Intellectual property that is developed *during* a partnership or joint development agreement, often collaboratively. The ownership of Foreground IP is a critical point of negotiation.

Founder An entrepreneur who is one of the original creators of a startup (although some key critical employees who join later can be given this title). Founders typically hold a large portion of the initial common stock and are responsible for setting the company's vision and building the initial team.

Fully Diluted A calculation of a company's total outstanding shares that assumes all convertible securities, such as stock options, warrants, and convertible notes, have been converted into common stock. This is the number VCs use to determine their ownership percentage.

Fundraising The process by which a startup, led by its founders, seeks and obtains capital from external investors (such as angels or VCs) to finance its operations and growth. This is often done in distinct stages, or "rounds."

Game Theory A field of study that analyzes how rational decision-makers interact in strategic situations where the outcome depends on the choices of others. It is often applied to understand the complex dynamics of negotiations in venture capital, including avoiding actions that could cause onerous terms in future transactions (a key reason for clean term sheets).

General Partners (GPs) The individuals who manage a venture capital fund, making investment decisions and actively working with portfolio companies. GPs are the most senior members of a VC fund and the key decision-makers.

Generalist VC A type of institutional venture capitalist that does not have a specific sector focus. They invest opportunistically across various industries, often relying on the diligence of sector-specialist co-investors.

Go-to-Market Partnership A formal strategic alliance where a startup uses the CVC's parent company's resources, such as its sales force, distribution channels, or brand, to sell its product and enter new markets. This is often one of the most valuable "strategic" returns a CVC can offer.

Golden Share A mechanism, often used by governments, where an entity takes a small stake in a company that grants it disproportionate rights, such as veto power over key decisions.

Herd Mentality A phenomenon in investing where participants follow the actions of a larger group or respected peers, rather than making independent decisions. It can be a powerful force in building momentum for a funding round.

Hurdle Rate A minimum rate of return that a venture capital fund must achieve before the General Partners can begin to receive their carried interest. It ensures LPs get a baseline return first.

Hybrid CVC A CVC firm that seeks to balance both strategic objectives for the parent company and strong financial returns for the fund. This is the most common CVC model.

Incubator A program designed to help very early-stage companies (often pre-product) develop their ideas and business models over a longer, less structured period than an accelerator.

Indemnification A contractual promise by one party to compensate another party for losses or damages incurred as a result of a specific event or breach of contract. In M&A deals, founders often have to indemnify the acquirer against any misrepresentations.

Institutional Venture Capital (VC) The traditional form of venture capital, where a fund is raised from institutional investors (LPs) and managed by professional investors (GPs) with a primary goal of financial return.

Intellectual Property (IP) A category of property that includes intangible creations of the human intellect, such as patents, copyrights, trademarks, and trade secrets. It is often a startup's most valuable asset.

Internal Champion An individual within the CVC or its parent company who takes personal responsibility for the success of a partnership or investment. This person advocates for the startup internally, navigates corporate bureaucracy, and is essential for getting a strategic deal approved.

Internal Rate of Return (IRR) A financial metric used to measure the profitability of an investment over time, expressed as an annualized percentage. It is a standard measure of performance for VC funds.

Investment Committee (IC) The group of senior partners at a VC firm who make the final decision on whether to approve an investment in a company.

Investors' Rights Agreement (IRA) A legal document in a financing that outlines the rights of investors, such as information rights, pro rata rights, and registration rights.

Joint Development Agreement (JDA) A contract between two or more parties to jointly develop a new product or technology. It outlines the scope of work, responsibilities, and, crucially, the ownership of any resulting IP.

Key Man Clause A "Key Man" or "Key Person" clause is a provision that makes an investment or partnership contingent on the continued involvement of specific, essential individuals, such as the founders. If a "key person" leaves the company, it can trigger a default or give the investor special rights.

Key Performance Indicators (KPIs) A set of quantifiable measurements used to gauge a company's performance over time. VCs use KPIs to track a startup's progress against its goals.

Lead Investor The VC firm that takes the primary role in a financing round. They typically invest the largest amount of capital, negotiate the valuation and terms, and often take a board seat.

Letter of Intent (LOI) A non-binding document that outlines the preliminary terms of a proposed transaction, such as an acquisition or a strategic partnership. It is similar to a term sheet and establishes the framework for definitive, binding legal agreements to be settled later.

Limited Partners (LPs) The passive investors in a venture capital fund, such as pension funds, endowments, and foundations, who provide the capital for GPs to invest.

Liquidation Preference A provision that gives preferred stockholders the right to be paid back their investment amount (often with a multiple) before common stockholders in the event of a sale or liquidation. More recent preferred stockholders usually have preference before older preferred shareholders in a "stacked preference."

Liquidity Event (See Exit). An event that allows investors and founders to convert their illiquid equity (stock) into cash. The most common liquidity events are an acquisition (M&A) or an Initial Public Offering (IPO).

M&A Pipeline A strategic objective for some CVCs, where the venture fund is used to build relationships with and monitor potential future acquisition targets for the parent company. This motivation can sometimes be in conflict with a startup's desire to remain independent or achieve a high, competitive exit.

Major Investor A term in a financing agreement that defines a threshold of investment (e.g., investing over $1 million) for an investor to receive certain enhanced rights, such as information rights or pro rata rights.

Management Fees An annual fee (typically 2% of committed capital) that a VC firm charges to its LPs to cover its operational expenses, such as salaries and office space.

Mentor An experienced and trusted advisor who provides guidance, industry knowledge, and network connections to a founder or startup. This relationship is typically informal and not based on direct compensation, distinguishing it from a paid "Advisor" who receives equity.

Micro VC A smaller, institutional venture capital firm that typically invests at the pre-seed and seed stages. These firms manage smaller funds (e.g., under $20 million) and often write smaller checks than larger, multi-stage VC firms.

Minimum Viable Product (MVP) A version of a new product which allows a team to collect the maximum amount of validated learning about customers with the least amount of effort.

Most Favored Nation (MFN) A provision in an agreement that ensures a party gets terms at least as good as any other party in a similar agreement. It is used to ensure fairness among investors.

Multiple on Invested Capital (MOIC) A performance metric that measures the total value (realized and unrealized) of an investment relative to the initial cost. It is calculated by dividing the total value by the amount of capital invested.

National Venture Capital Association (NVCA) A venture capital trade association that has helped standardize legal documents for venture financings. Their model legal documents are widely used in the industry.

Non-Disclosure Agreement (NDA) A legal contract that establishes confidentiality and prohibits the sharing of proprietary information between parties.

Not Invented Here (NIH) Syndrome A common cultural mindset within large corporations that causes them to be resistant to external ideas or technologies, preferring their own internal R&D. CVCs and innovation outposts are often created to act as a bridge to overcome this internal bias.

Option Pool (See Employee Pool). This is a percentage of the company's stock reserved for issuing stock options to future employees, advisors, and consultants. This pool is a critical part of a term sheet negotiation, as its size directly impacts the dilution of all existing shareholders.

Oversubscribed Round An investment round where there is more interest from investors to deploy capital than the startup intends to raise. Common for "hot" startups. Some investors will need to be turned down, and others will compete for allocation.

Parent Company (or Corporate Parent) The large corporation that owns and funds a CVC arm. The parent company's strategic goals, financial health, and internal politics are key drivers of a CVC's behavior and interests.

Pari Passu A Latin phrase meaning "on equal footing," which signifies that two or more securities or investors have the same rights. For example, investors in the same series of preferred stock are typically pari passu with each other in a liquidation preference. However, it can sometimes be applied to investors across different rounds sharing liquidation preference.

Pay-to-Play A provision that requires existing investors to participate in a subsequent, often difficult, funding round to avoid a penalty. If they fail to "pay to play," they can lose their anti-dilution protection or even have their preferred stock converted to common stock. This is a term usually applied when existing investors are reluctant to continue to support a portfolio company and have written it off.

Phantom Carry A bonus structure for CVC professionals that is designed to mimic the financial incentives of carried interest. It links their compensation to the fund's performance without granting them actual equity in the fund.

Pilot Purgatory A common and frustrating failure mode for startups working with large corporations, where a successful pilot program fails to convert into a large-scale commercial contract. The project gets "stuck in purgatory," perpetually entering small-scale pilot programs with companies without them ever converting to large-scale deployments that generate meaningful revenue.

Pitch Deck A brief presentation, often 10–20 slides, used to provide an audience with a quick and compelling overview of a business plan, vision, and team. It is the primary tool used by founders to generate interest from investors.

Platform Team A team of non-investment professionals at a VC or CVC firm (often called a "Portfolio Services" or "Strategic Partnership" team) dedicated to providing operational help to portfolio companies.

In an institutional VC, this team usually consists of marketing, government affairs, or HR assistance. In a CVC, this team is crucial, as they are often the "bridge" responsible for facilitating connections and partnerships with the parent company's business units.

Portfolio Company A startup that a venture capital firm has invested in. VCs refer to their investments as their "portfolio."

Post-Money Valuation The value of a company immediately *after* it has received an investment. It is calculated as the Pre-Money Valuation plus the amount of new capital invested, and is usually the number showcased in news reports.

Pre-Money Valuation The value of a company *before* it receives a new round of investment. It is a key term negotiated in financing.

Preferred Stock A class of stock that venture capital investors purchase, which has superior rights and protections compared to the common stock held by founders and employees. These rights often include a liquidation preference and protective provisions.

Priced Round A financing round where the company's valuation is explicitly determined and investors purchase shares at a fixed price per share. This is distinct from a convertible note or SAFE round.

Principal (Title) A mid-level investment professional at a VC firm, typically senior to an Associate but junior to a Partner. They generally hold sway in an investment committee, but not a vote.

Private Placement Memorandum (PPM) A long and formal legal document prepared by bankers (should a startup choose to use them) to solicit investors. It is much more detailed than a pitch deck and formally discloses business details, financial statements, and key risks to comply with securities laws.

Pro-Rata Rights The right, but not the obligation, for an investor to maintain their initial percentage ownership in a company by participating in subsequent funding rounds.

Proof-of-Concept (PoC) A small-scale project or pilot designed to test the feasibility and demonstrate the potential of a new product or idea, often with a potential customer.

Protective Provisions A set of rights granted to preferred stockholders that gives them a veto over certain major corporate actions. These often include the right to block a sale of the company, the issuance of new, more senior stock, or a change in the company's business.

Pulling a Term Sheet The act of a VC revoking a term sheet after it has been issued but before the deal has closed. This is considered a serious breach of etiquette in Silicon Valley and can cause significant reputational damage to a VC fund.

Redemption Rights A right that allows an investor to demand that the company buy back their shares after a certain period of time.

Reserves The amount of capital a VC fund "reserves" or sets aside for future, follow-on investments in its existing portfolio companies. A CVC's policy on reserves is a critical indicator of its long-term commitment.

Retraction Rights A right that allows a CVC to sell its shares back to the company for a nominal sum (e.g., $1) in the event of a scandal or major reputational damage to the startup. This is a highly unusual and founder-unfriendly term.

Right of First Offer (ROFO) A contractual right that requires the holder of the right to be offered a deal (such as an acquisition or partnership) before it is offered to any other party.

Right of First Refusal (ROFR) A contractual right that gives its holder the option to match the terms of a deal that the company has negotiated with a third party.

Runway The amount of time a startup has before it runs out of money, assuming its current revenue and expenses. It is typically measured in months.

Simple Agreement for Future Equity (SAFE) A type of convertible security, pioneered by YCombinator, that allows a startup to raise capital without setting a valuation. It is a warrant to purchase equity in a future priced round.

Sand Hill Road A street in Menlo Park, California, that is famous for its high concentration of top-tier venture capital firms. It is often used as a synonym for the venture capital industry itself.

Secondary Market Usually organized by a broker, a secondary market is a way for employees and investors to sell private shares in a company to each other outside of normal financing. These transactions usually require approval from the Board of Directors.

Seed Round The first official equity funding stage for a new company. It typically represents the first significant capital a startup raises to fund its initial product development and team building.

Series A, B, C, etc. The named stages of venture capital financing that follow the initial seed round. Each round is typically larger than the last and is used to fund a new phase of growth.

Side Letter A supplementary agreement that grants specific, tailored rights to one or more investors that are not included in the main financing documents shared by all investors. It is a key tool for CVCs to secure strategic terms.

Signaling Effect The phenomenon where the participation of a high-profile or well-respected investor in a funding round increases the appeal of the startup to other investors. It signals that the company has passed a high bar for diligence.

Spin-Out A new, independent startup company that is created from an internal project, technology, or team "spun out" of a larger corporation. These are often the product of internal innovation labs or EIR programs.

Stacked Preference A liquidation preference structure where different series of preferred stock are layered on top of each other (e.g., Series B gets its money back, then Series A, then common). This is the standard in most venture deals.

Strategic Fit The measure of how well a startup's technology, product, or market aligns with the strategic priorities and business units of the CVC's parent company. For most CVCs, demonstrating a strong "strategic fit" is just as important, if not more so, than demonstrating pure financial potential.

Strategic Investor An investor whose primary motivation for investing is to gain a strategic advantage for their own business, such as access to new technology or market intelligence. Financial returns are often a secondary priority for a purely strategic investor. This term, however, has often been used interchangeably with CVC, especially when referring to the syndicate of a round, for example, "We have an institutional lead and a few strategic follows."

Stock Option A contract that gives an employee or advisor the right, but not the obligation, to purchase a share of company stock at a fixed price (the "strike price") at a future date. Options are the primary tool used to grant equity from the employee pool.

Stock Purchase Agreement (SPA) A definitive legal document that governs the sale of stock in a company. It details the terms of the transaction, including the price, number of shares, and representations and warranties.

Strategic Bridge Round A small financing round, typically composed of CVCs or strategic partners, raised between larger priced rounds. It is framed as a validation of the company's commercial traction rather than a sign of financial distress.

Strike Price (See Basis of Stock Option). The pre-determined, fixed price per share that an employee must pay to "exercise" (or purchase) their vested stock options. This price is typically set by the Fair Market Value (FMV) of the common stock at the time the option is granted.

Super Angel An angel investor who invests larger amounts of capital, often on a full-time basis, and sometimes manages a small, informal fund. They bridge the gap between traditional angel investors and institutional Micro VCs.

Syndicate A group of investors who join together to invest in a single funding round. A strong syndicate can bring a diverse set of skills and networks to a startup.

Synergy The corporate concept that the combination of the startup's technology and the corporation's resources (like distribution or data) will create a combined value greater than the sum of its parts. CVCs are often required to demonstrate "synergy" to their parent company to justify their investments.

Technology Debt (Tech Debt) Technology debt is the implied long-term cost of rework and complexity that accumulates when a team chooses an easy, expedient technical solution now instead of a better, more scalable approach that would take longer to implement.

Term Sheet A non-binding document that outlines the basic terms and conditions of an investment. It serves as the template and foundation for the definitive legal documents.

Valuation The process of determining the current worth of a company, or the value itself. In financing, the "pre-money valuation" is a key point of negotiation between the founder and investors, as it determines the price per share.

Valuation Insensitive A term describing an investor, often a purely strategic CVC, who is less focused on negotiating a low valuation than on securing access to the technology or partnership. This can sometimes lead to a CVC being willing to pay a higher price than an institutional, financially focused VC. This is where the term "dumb money" originates, as these investors are not seeking strong financial return, and therefore may not be aligned with the long-term growth of the company.

Vanity Metrics A set of metrics a startup shares that projects their business in a favorable light. These can often be retention, engagement, or revenue growth metrics that show the strongest growth and excite investors the most.

Venture Capital (VC) A form of private equity financing provided by venture capital firms to startups and early-stage companies that are deemed to have high growth potential.

Venture Partner (Title) A part-time or senior advisory role at a VC firm, often held by an experienced entrepreneur or executive who helps source deals and mentor portfolio companies. A Venture Partner does not have the same full-time management responsibilities or economic share as a GP.

Venture Scout (Title) An individual, often an entrepreneur or well-connected industry expert, who is not a full-time employee of a VC firm but is paid to source potential investment opportunities for them. Scouts act as the firm's "eyes and ears," often receiving a finder's fee or a share of the profits if a deal they source is successful.

Veto Rights The right for an investor to block certain corporate actions, even if they do not have a majority of votes on the board or among shareholders. These are typically reserved for major decisions.

Voting Agreement A legal document in a financing that governs how investors and key common stockholders will vote their shares on certain matters, such as the election of board members.

Waterfall (or Distribution Waterfall) This is the legal and financial model that dictates the exact order and method of how proceeds are distributed to all shareholders through a "Stacked Preference" after a liquidity event, like a sale. It ensures that preferred stockholders receive their liquidation preferences in order before any money "flows down" to the common stockholders.

Window Shopping/Window on Technology A common strategic motivation for a CVC, where the primary goal of investing is to gain early insights and market intelligence into emerging technologies and trends. This can sometimes lead to "performative diligence" with no real intent to invest.

Write-Off/Write-Down An accounting action taken by an investor to reduce the value of a portfolio company on their own books, often triggered by a "down round" or poor performance. A "write-down" is a partial reduction in value, while a "write-off" is a complete reduction to zero, effectively declaring the investment a total loss.

Warrant A security, similar to a stock option, that gives the holder the right to purchase company stock at a fixed price (the "strike price") for a defined period. Warrants are often used as a "sweetener" for strategic partners, rather than for employee compensation.

Index

For Product Safety Concerns and Information please contact our EU representative GPSR@taylorandfrancis.com Taylor & Francis Verlag GmbH, Kaufingerstraße 24, 80331 München, Germany